Forgotten Voices

Forgotten Voices

POWER AND AGENCY IN COLONIAL AND POSTCOLONIAL LIBYA

ALI ABDULLATIF AHMIDA

Routledge
Taylor & Francis Group
New York   London

Published in 2005 by
Routledge
Taylor & Francis Group
270 Madison Avenue
New York, NY 10016

Published in Great Britain by
Routledge
Taylor & Francis Group
2 Park Square
Milton Park, Abingdon
Oxon OX14 4RN

Printed in the United States of America on acid-free paper
10 9 8 7 6 5 4 3 2 1

International Standard Book Number-10: 0-415-94986-6 (Hardcover) 0-415-94987-4 (Softcover)
International Standard Book Number-13: 978-0-415-94986-6 (Hardcover) 978-0-415-94987-3 (Softcover)

Library of Congress Cataloging-in-Publication Data

Ahmida, Ali Abdullatif, 1953–
    Forgotten voices: power and agency in colonial and postcolonial Libya / Ali Abdullatif Ahmida.
        p. cm.
    Includes bibliographical references and index.
    ISBN 0-415-94986-6 (hb : alk. paper) -- ISBN 0-415-94987-4 (pb : alk. paper)
    1. Libya--politics and government--19th century. 2. Libya--politics and government--20th century.
I. Title.
DT233.A35 2005   2005004312

Taylor & Francis Group
is the Academic Division of T&F Informa plc.

Visit the Taylor & Francis Web site at
http://www.taylorandfrancis.com

and the Routledge Web site at
http://www.routledge-ny.com

For my wife Beth,
and young children Haneen and Zach

CONTENTS

ACKNOWLEDGMENTS

I wish to thank several institutions and people who have given me support, valuable criticism, and suggestions during the last three years of working on this book. I am grateful to my Routledge/Taylor & Francis editors Karen Wolny and Rob Tempio. Karen saw potential in my original proposal, and Rob was patient and understanding of my requests for more deadline extensions for completing the book due to the death of my mother and my responsibility as a teacher and a father of two young children.

Chapters 5 and 6 of the book were published before and have been updated. I would like to thank both Palgrave and Heinemann Presses for permission to print an updated version of the two chapters. Chapter 5 appeared originally as "Identity, Alienation, and Cultural Encounter in Postcolonial Libyan Literature" in my edited book, *Beyond Colonialism and Nationalism in the Maghrib: History, Culture and Politics* (Palgrave, 2000). Chapter 6 appeared as "Libya, the Jamahiriyya: Historical and Social Origins of a Populist State" in the Abdi and Ahmed Samatar edited book, *The African State: Reconsiderations* (Heinemann, 2002). Also, I am grateful to my friend Ms. Frances Stickles and the Libyan Studies Center in Tripoli, Libya for permission to include copies of photos in this book.

In Libya, I continued to find support and assistance at the Center of Libyan Studies in Tripoli. I am grateful to my good friend Mohammed Jerary, the director of the Center and the Center's staff, especially Salem Kubti, Nasr al-Din Jerary, Mahmood el-Deek, and Ghada al-Zaruq, who assisted me during my short visits to Libya while I researched material for this book. At the Libyan Studies Center I was given access to files of the original collected oral history project and the historical archives. My brother, Salem Abdullatif Ahmida, provided logistical support in all of my visits.

My late mother, Mabruka, died three years ago. She inspired me to continue writing about the history of the forgotten Libyan people under colonialism. A proud, dignified, and strong Libyan woman, my mother was born in the harsh desert exile of northern Chad, never attended school, and got married at the early age of sixteen. I was fortunate to listen to her tell her story struggling for survival in her early childhood and learn from her tolerance and generosity toward others. I miss our weekly long distance telephone conversations, her quick tongue, and great sense of humor.

In the United States, I would like to thank librarians Janice Beal and Brenda Austin, media specialist Holly Haywood and my assistant Denise Gendron at University of New England for their assistance and support. Two good work-studies students, Ethan Daly and Shawny Donohue, assisted me in researching the state of the field of comparative fascism. Khaled Mattawa helped me translate the long folk epic poem "Mabi Marad" written by Rajab Buhwaish al-Minifi in the terrible Agaila Fascist concentration camp (1930). Rifa'at Abou-El-Haj and Peter Gran provided critical comments on an earlier original proposal and chapter 4 of the book and helped me see the larger comparative and global implications of Libyan history. Thanks to Janet Dinsmore and Susan McHugh who proofread and made valuable editorial suggestions. While many individuals helped me gather my research archival data and oral interviews and articulate my arguments, responsibility for the final draft remains mine alone.

My wife, Beth, and two young children, Haneen and Zach, have lived with this book for three years. Beth has continued to provide support and encouragement, and Haneen and Zach with their delightful spirits have reminded me that books are not an end but about real people and the larger world.

A NOTE ON THE TRANSLITERATION

The proper names of persons and places are spelled according to the Arabic transliteration system followed by the *International Journal of Middle East Studies*. Turkish names, persons, and administrative terms are spelled according to Arabic translation, as most of the sources of this study were written in Arabic. Exceptions to this system of transliteration are commonplace names or proper names that are widely used, such as *Fezzan* instead of *Fazzan* and *Abdulnabi Bilkhayre* instead of *Abu al-Khayr*.

INTRODUCTION

In the past three decades, mainstream academic scholarship on the Arab and Muslim world has been challenged by a new generation of scholars using methods and concepts borrowed from neo-Marxism, feminism, postmodernism, and postcolonial analysis. This book on Libyan social and cultural history is inspired by my personal background, and influenced by theoretical debates within these critical perspectives—particularly subaltern studies, new Ottoman social history, and orientalist debates.

I was born in central Libya and raised in the southern region of Fezzan. Both my grandparents and parents experienced Italy's colonial rule of Libya firsthand. My grandfather, Ali, was a militant opponent of Italian colonialism for ten years, with the result that his wife, my grandmother Aisha, gave birth to my mother in a harsh desert exile (northern Chad). She died without being able to return to her homeland, and my other grandmother, Mabruka, lost two children to famine. This heritage forms the deepest part of my sensibility about social history, although I also became disillusioned with the nationalist military regimes in the Arab world and their security approach to law, dissent, pluralism, education, and history.

In the early 1980s, I came to the United States for graduate school. Most of my research in the past twenty years has focused on mapping colonial and nationalist political models and analyzing the social history of the Maghrib (especially Libya) during the second half of the nineteenth and first half of the twentieth centuries. This book continues and revises work undertaken in *The Making of Modern Libya: State Formation, Colonialization, and Resistance, 1830–1932* (State University of New York Press, 1994) and my edited collection on mapping North

African scholarship, *Beyond Colonialism and Nationalism in the Maghrib: History, Culture, and Politics* (Palgrave Press, 2000). Most chapters in this book are revisions of papers presented at academic conferences in North America, Europe, and Africa in the past ten years. Topics cover the early nineteenth century to the end of the twentieth century.

From the nineteenth into the twentieth century, the study of Libya and the larger Maghrib's history was dominated by a colonialist mindset. It was not until the mid-twentieth century that nationalist movements leading the fight for independence assumed state power and produced their own historiographies. Two forces—colonialism and nationalism—not only shaped the political and social life of the region, but also invented their own concepts and theories of scholarly legitimation. Their dominance demonstrates the fact that the production of knowledge is often circumstantial and constrained within institutional and social boundaries. Because modern social science developed in response to European colonial problems, and at a point when Europe dominated the world, it was inevitable that Western social science reflected European choices with respect to subjects, theories, and epistemology. A subsequent Maghribi nationalist historiography has challenged French, Spanish, Italian, and British colonialist analyses, but still accepts colonialist definitions of the Maghrib, periodization of history, the model of the nation-state, and notion of progress.

The very term *Maghrib*, applied only to French colonies of North Africa and Libya, was invented and defined by Italy at the turn of the twentieth century. Contemporary nationalist elites in the region have often followed this definition, consequently reducing the larger Muslim Maghrib to include only its French colonies of Algeria, Tunisia, and Morocco. If regional boundaries were carefully reassessed by analyzing precolonial political traditions, the Muslim Maghrib would encompass territory from western Egypt to the Atlantic and to the Saharan frontiers of Bilad al-Sudan. Nationalist historians have also uncritically accepted the colonial periodization of the region's history into precolonial, colonial, and postcolonial. An alternative approach might be to look at internal changes prior to colonialism, such as modernization of the Ottoman state, local movements such as the Sanusiyya, or creation of the states of Ali Bey al-Kabir in Egypt and Hamuda Pasha in Tunisia.

Recent social challenges from political Islamic movements in the Maghribi states indicate that they have been going through a crisis of legitimacy and relevancy. This challenge, whether in Algeria, Tunisia, Egypt, or more recently in Libya, is not unique; the nation-states in Europe are going through their own crises. Eric Hobsbawm and David Held, among others, have pointed out the historical mythology of nation-state nationalism and noted the forces of global capitalism transcending national boundaries.[1] The crisis of the Maghribi nation-state suggests that most Middle East scholars have taken the claims of the nation-state and Arab nationalism for granted. In my view, the best studies of the Ottoman and Moroccan empires and the rise of nationalism do not spell out a modality of nationalism while ignoring the Islamic alternative.

The objective of *Forgotten Voices* is to rethink the history of colonial and nationalist analyses of modern Libya. It critiques the current scholarship on Libya, which focuses on Qadhdhafi—ignoring Libyan society and culture—and argues that, under colonialism and postcolonialism, Libyan society confronted contradictions of modernity, genocide, the nation-state, and alienation. This study assumes that both subjective individual perspectives and objective documentary material are essential to understanding the making of history. The chapters of this book consequently examine the social processes that produce and condition the voices of ordinary Libyan people in response to pressures and opportunity, with particular attention to peasants, tribesmen, women, slaves, and victims of fascist concentration camps. The book recognizes that while the context of power affects people, human agency matters. Only by analyzing both can social history be captured.[2]

Chapter 1 reexamines the origins of state formation and regionalism under the Ottoman Empire and how diverse regionalism affected social and political movement. It demystifies why the Libyan people reacted differently to the Italian colonial conquest in 1911. Chapter 2 analyzes the significance of recently discovered local materials about the state of Awlad Muhammad in Fezzan, which was defeated by the state of Qaramanli in 1813. Chapter 3 disputes the "modernization" and anthropological view of colonial Libya as dominated by ageless traditions and ideology, such as religion and kinship organization. Challenging the denial of a class structure in Italian colonies, the preceding analysis provides empirical and qualitative evidence of social class as an economic and cultural reality in the politics of resistance. This moral economy approach offers a new interpretation of the complex roles of tribe, region, class, and state formation, which conditioned Libyan reactions to colonialism. Chapter 4 maps out the historiography of Italian fascism and demonstrates how the silence of scholars on the genocide in Libya has led to the perception of Italian fascism as benign, or a lesser evil than Germany's. It introduces the oral history and poetry of Libyans who survived the concentration camps between 1929 and 1934. Chapter 5 analyzes the trilogy of the Libyan writer Ahmad Ibrahim al-Faqih, focusing on identity, cultural encounter, and alienation. The

final chapter sums up the burden of colonial and nationalist dominance by examining the origins, politics, and limits of the Jamahiriyya
state between 1977 and 2003.

My final objective is to defend civil society—Libyan society—by
recovering its diverse and dynamic social and cultural history as a
world history and not as an exceptional, unique case. This objective
required a multidisciplinary approach that includes epistemological
questions from political theory and historical sociology about the study
of agency and power.

I approach Libyan social and cultural history with respect to its own
dynamics and not as a footnote in the history of colonialism, modernity, and capitalism. Listening to the voices of history means that the
views of the majority of ordinary illiterate tribesmen, peasants, migrant
labor, women, and slaves are taken seriously. Their views will not be
found in the elitist colonial and nationalist state archives but in oral
traditions, songs, folk poetry, and proverbs. Inevitably I found myself
relying on personal, political, and literary history. I had to do the work
of a historian by researching the state archives, an anthropologist by
conducting oral interviews, and a literary critic by educating myself
about folk poetry so that I could make sense of the history of a people
without history as they were ignored or misrepresented by colonial and
postcolonial elites.

1

FROM THE OTTOMANS TO THE ITALIANS: A POLITICAL ECONOMY APPROACH TO STATE FORMATION IN NINETEENTH-CENTURY LIBYA

We can no longer be content with writing only the history of the victorious elites, or with detailing the subjugation of the dominated ethnic groups. Social historians and historical sociologists have shown that the common people were as much agents in historical process as they were its victims and silent witnesses.

> Eric W. Wolf, *Europe and the People without History*

It should be known that differences of conditions among people are the result of different ways in which they make their living.

> Ibn Khaldun, fourteenth-century historian

Men make their own history, but they do not make it just as they please; they do not make it under circumstances chosen by themselves, but under circumstances directly encountered, given and transmitted from the past.

> Karl Marx, *The 18th Brumaire of Louis Bonaparte*

This chapter reassesses the nature of the Ottoman state in Libya from 1835 to Italy's invasion of Libya in 1911. While most historians of that period, including Tahir Ahmad al-Zawi, Abdullah Ibrahim, and Lisa Anderson, argue that Tarabulus al-Gharb—the name of the country and city of Tripoli as nineteenth-century Libya was known—was a powerful central government in control of the hinterland by 1860,[1] their analyses are based on dynastic or modernization theories. These theories ignore the salience of regional political economies. It is my contention that Libya's three major regions in the nineteenth century developed distinct political economies resulting from unique ecologies and the inability of the central state to control them. I argue that studies neglecting the significance of geography, commercial relations, and social classes are flawed because they limit our understanding of the dynamics of state formation and, consequently, the colonial period in Libya.

This chapter uses a political economy approach to state formation—an approach that emphasizes modes of production focusing on property relations, ecology, social classes, and ideology. It does not deny the impact of ideology, leadership, and nationalism, but interprets their development against a materialist background and assumes a mutual interaction between economy and ideology. To illustrate, three major issues will be addressed: (1) the rural–urban markets' integration in Tripolitania; (2) the decline of Fezzan's political economy in the second half of the last century; and (3) the rise of Cyrenaica's economy in spite of the marginality of its urban markets. This approach considers each region to have a political economy of its own, rather than assuming a single unit of analysis, the province of Ottoman Libya known as Tarabulus al-Gharb.

GEOGRAPHY: THE SOURCE OF AUTONOMY

Tarabulus al-Gharb under Ottoman rule was made up of three distinct geographical regions: Tripolitania in the west, Fezzan in the south, and Cyrenaica in the east. As a desert country without rivers, the topography discouraged communication among the three regions. Even along parts of the Mediterranean coast in the Gulf of Syrte, the desert and the sea come face to face, forming a natural barrier between Tripolitania and Cyrenaica. Rainfall is scant and inconsistent. The coast of Tripolitania averages 300 mm annually, the Green Mountain of northern Cyrenaica receives 500 to 600 mm, and Fezzan and Southern Cyrenaica receive less than 10 mm.[2] Only 5 percent of the entire country is suitable for cultivation, limiting settled agriculture to the coast of Tripolitania, parts of the Jfara plain and western mountains, the Marj plain in Cyrenaica, and the oases of Fezzan and Cyrenaica up to the middle of the century (see Figure 1.1). Two conclusions emerge from a consideration of Libyan geography. One is that pastoralism persisted from the time of the Hilali nomadic conquest in the eleventh century in response to natural ecological conditions (i.e., soil, rainfall, and climate), socioeconomic factors (i.e., a simple technology), and the inability of the tributary state to settle tribes prior to 1860.[3] The second points to the significance of regionalism. The country's vast size and division by a large desert encouraged development of distinct regional characteristics, including unique urban markets and local political organizations. Far from being able to subdue hinterland tribes, which were mobile and militarized, the city of Tripoli could not control those who resisted or escaped into the desert.

The agropastoral economy was limited to herding animals and cultivating grain in rainy seasons but drought and famine occurred frequently.[4] Trade across the Sahara with the more stable agrarian political economies of Europe, the Near East, and central and western Africa provided a more reliable source of income. Libya's strategic location as the closest region to western Africa across the Mediterranean meant that three of the five major trade routes went through Libya.[5]

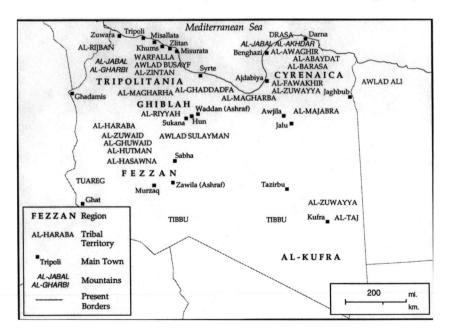

Figure 1.1 Map of Libya: main towns, tribal territories, and regions (1910–1911).

Two routes cut through western Libya: one through Tripoli, Fezzan, Kawar, and Bornu, and one through Tripoli, Ghadamis, Ghat, Air, and Kano. The third crossed eastern Libya from Benghazi, through Kufra to Wadai.[6]

The trans-Sahara trade was established during the Roman Empire—a mercantile trade based on the exchange of luxury goods such as cloth, ivory, ostrich feathers, and gold as well as goatskins, guns, and slaves. European merchants sought markets for exporting cloth and guns; western African aristocracies desired these goods, and local Libyan economies profited by taxing the caravans to guarantee their free passage into tribal lands. Local tribesmen also worked as guides and benefited from other exchanges with the Europeans.

Organized regionally in Tripolitania, Fezzan, and Cyrenaica, the Sahara trade created strong alliances between the merchant class and tribal confederations such as the Qaramanli, Awlad Muhammad, and the Sanusiyya order, which came to dominate the trade. It flourished throughout western Libya until the 1880s, but as French and British colonialism advanced into western and central Africa, it began to decline. However, a third trade route through Cyrenaica continued to the turn of the twentieth century.[7]

The development of rural and urban markets in each region conditioned social and political loyalties. Tripolitanian urban markets were located mainly in the city of Tripoli (the center of the Sahara trade), and the agropastoral produced a surplus from rural areas and Fezzan.[8] Fezzan also prospered as a market for the merchants of the Sahara trade, pushing the population of towns such as Murzaq, Ghadamis, Ghat, and Sukana to between 10,000 and 12,000 by the 1880s.[9] Locally, the state of Awlad Muhammad emerged to organize the trade along the Sahara, which lasted from 1550 to 1813.[10] Cyrenaica, however, had no real urban market. By 1860, Benghazi and Darnah each had a population of only 5,000.[11] Through the end of the nineteenth century, the natural urban market for the tribes of the hinterland was northwestern Egypt.[12]

Cyrenaica's autonomy, beyond the reach of Tripoli, continued even after 1835 when the regency expanded its control into rural Tripolitania and Fezzan. Its independence was furthered by a strong militarized confederation of tribes, and the rise of the religion-based Sanusi order during the second half of the nineteenth century. The combination of religious, social, and commercial components, along with an already elaborate tribal organization, transformed Cyrenaica into a de facto state.[13]

A HISTORY OF TRIBUTARY RELATIONSHIPS

Early Ottoman society was dominated by tributary relationships. The Ottoman army conquered the region in 1551 and incorporated its tribes into a tributary system that supported the Ottoman regency's economy and dominance. The regency lived on taxes and tributes from urban and coastal areas, while strong militarized tribes collected tributes from peasants and client tribes—as in the case of the Mahamid in Tripolitania, the Awlad Sulayman in Fezzan, the Tuareg in southwest Fezzan, and the Sa'adi in Cyrenaica. In 1711, an ambitious Turkish military officer, Ahmad Qaramanli, founded an autonomous dynasty ruled by his descendants until 1835. Extending its authority over Fezzan, the Qaramanlis crushed the state of Awlad Muhammad in 1811 and profited from Fezzan's rich trading revenues.[14]

While the tributary system fed the rise of the Qaramanli, it also led to their downfall. Pressured in the 1820s by the French and British navies to stop imposing tributes on European ships in exchange for free passage, Yusuf Qaramanli began to borrow from the local and foreign traders. This policy led to the state's bankruptcy when Yusuf Qaramanli could not pay his debts to French and British traders. France and Britain responded by blockading Tripoli, forcing Qaramanli to sign treaties in 1830 and 1832, which not only called for paying his debts, but also guaranteed numerous privileges for European traders in the hinterland, including the ability to trade freely, have their own courts, and be exempted from paying major tributes to the state.[15]

In desperation, Yusuf Qaramanli imposed new taxes and lifted the exemption for paying taxes previously granted to the Cologhli class—descendants of the sixteenth- and seventeenth-century Turkish Janissary,[16] who had become police and landlords. The Cologhli rebelled and rallied around his grandson Muhammad. Yusuf, who was old by 1832, resigned in favor of his son, Ali. The dynastic crisis turned into civil war with tribal chiefs and Europeans siding with different rivals,[17] and gave the Ottoman imperial authority a chance to take control of the regency. With France advancing into neighboring Tunisia in 1881, Tarabulus al-Gharb became the last Ottoman province in North Africa.

A WEAK STATE STRUCTURE

The Ottomans inherited a weak to nonexistent central state structure. Neither feudal like western Europe nor similar to Asiatic modes of production, the regency had no authority over the hinterland and only small garrisons in Fezzan's and Cyrenaica's major towns. There was no administrative process beyond the army to collect taxes from traders, peasants, and tribes, and unlike feudal Europe, the agropastoral tribes in the hinterland had their own armies of warrior lords who monopolized the use of arms. Further, armed tribesmen could always escape into the desert.

No large landowning class existed. While private property was held in urban areas and Saharan oases, it was not stable. In the hinterland, equipment and animals were individually owned but land was owned collectively.[18] The peasantry in Tripolitania and Fezzan cultivated land for their own families or worked for landlords as sharecroppers. Cyrenaica had no actual peasantry.[19]

While the country's economy was oriented toward self-sufficiency, tribes were not completely separate or isolated. Pastoralists traded with peasants, and both took part in larger tributary relationships. In fact, the Libyan social history of cooperation between pastoralists and peasants is in conflict with the views of scholars, such as Perry Anderson, regarding a purely pastoralist mode of production.[20] Within each tribe, slaves, clients, and artisans existed, and Libyan tribes did pay some taxes to the regency.

These complex divisions refute the segmentary model propounded by Evans-Pritchard and Ernest Gellner. Especially if one considers the larger panoply of trade, clients, and states' relationships, it is clear that tribal segments were unequal and a complex stratified structure was in place. Some tribes, like the Sa'adi, for example, benefited from owning the best land and water resources, while others—client tribes like the Murabtin in Cyrenaica—were forced to pay tributes. Some tribal chiefs were exempted from taxes; others paid.[21] Enforcement of policies was inconsistent at best. While the state relied on its army and shifting loyalties of coastal tribes, hinterland tribes and peasants had their own political alliances or *sufuf* to protect local land ownership from other tribes and the state. [22]

1835: OTTOMAN STATE FORMATION

Around 1835, four major factors began to affect the fragmented social structure of Tarabulus al-Gharb. The first involved the Ottoman's state-formation efforts (see Table 1.1); the second, European commercial penetration of rural Tripolitania; the third, the decline of the Sahara trade through western Libya; and the fourth, the rise of the Sanusi order in the Sahara and Cyrenaica.

TABLE 1.1 State Formation in Tarabulus al Gharb [Libya] between the Sixteenth and Twentieth Centuries

1551	Regency of the Ottoman Empire	1911
1550	The State of Awlad Muhammad in Fezzan	1813
1711	The Qaramanli State	1835
1843	The Sanusiyya in Cyrenaica and the Sahara	1932
1911	The Italian Colonial State	1943
1918	The Tripolitanian Republic	1920
1943	British and French Administrations	1951
1951	The Sanusi Monarchy	1969
1969	The Republic	1977
1977	The Jamahiriyya	Present

Ottoman imperial policy was directed toward building a strong central state through tax revenues in order to combat European expansion. This goal required subduing strong tribal confederations in the hinterland and abolishing all tax exemptions. This objective, in turn, required the creation of a strong enough army to crush autonomous tribes, a new bureaucracy to conduct state policy, the settling of nomadic tribes, the protection of trade, and the creation of an educational system to provide the administrators, teachers, judges, and others needed to run the new bureaucracy.[23] It was an ambitious mission and one not easily accomplished.

Defeat of the two major tribal *sufuf* confederations—the Mahamid and the Awlad Sulayman in Tripolitania and Fezzan, respectively—took the Ottoman army almost 20 years. The Mahamid, who had enjoyed tax-exempt status under the Qaramanli, refused to give up their privilege, rebelling against the state under their charismatic chief Ghuma between 1835 and 1858. The Awlad Sulayman, led by 'Abd al-Jalil who controlled trade through Fezzan, refused to obey the state without major concessions. The rebellions finally ended with the killing of 'Abd al-Jalil in 1842 and Ghuma in 1858.[24]

In 1858, the Ottomans instituted a land code requiring registration of land owned by individuals. The policy was aimed at collecting taxes directly from property owners rather than through tribal or notable intermediaries who amassed wealth from taking a share of land revenues. While resistance continued for several decades, urban hegemony over the countryside began to appear by the end of the nineteenth century as rural Tripolitania became tied politically to the central state in Tripoli. Major tribes in eastern Tripolitania began to settle, with tribal chiefs and urban notables registering land to themselves and moving to fill most of the state's mid-level bureaucratic positions. It was clear that the political economy had begun shifting from tributary relationships toward a capitalist commercial structure.

EUROPEAN COMMERCIAL PENETRATION

Merchant capital has existed in the economy since 1800. During the Napoleonic wars in the 1800s, the regency supplied grain and meat to the British navy, [25] and during the same period, two British companies held a monopoly over the collection and shipping of esparto (*halfa* in Arabic), a grass grown in Tripolitania.[26] Many tribesmen worked, in fact, as wage laborers for the esparto trade, forming the beginnings of a small working class in an export economy. [27] In addition, although the Sahara trade in luxury goods was partially controlled by tribal customs and bartering, European merchants invested in and helped shape the luxury goods trade.

Decline of the Sahara trade. With European colonial expansion into central Africa in the 1880s and the wars of Rabih al-Zubair around Lake Chad, the Sahara trade declined drastically. [28] The loss of trade forced Tripolitanian tribesmen and peasants to migrate to urban areas and French Tunisia, where they found work with European firms and in colonial construction.[29] As Table 1.2 shows, Tripoli city and other Tripolitanian towns swelled with these rural migrants,[30] a process that accelerated when the Bank of Rome began investing in Libyan agriculture in 1907.[31]

I would classify Libyan merchants who worked for European banks and firms as compradore (intermediary) class. Compradore merchants and notables unhappy with the Ottoman administration found work with the bank.[32]

While the economy of Tripolitania was modified and transformed by the loss of the Sahara trade, Fezzan's economy was devastated. Once booming and wealthy towns bustling with caravans, craft industries, and merchants from throughout north and central Africa

TABLE 1.2 The Population of Tripolitanian Towns between 1883 and 1911

Town	1883	1911
Tripoli city	20,000	29,644
Zawiya	8,000	28,842
al-Azizayah	9,000	26,899
Zlitan	20,000	38,042
Misurata	20,000	39,029

became marginal villages[33] as merchants and peasants joined the migration to Tripolitania's coastal towns or French Tunisia's employment opportunities.[34]

RISE OF THE SANUSI ORDER

Only rural Cyrenaica remained separated from Tripoli in the early 1800s. Its strong tribal confederation continued to trade with the Egyptians over land, especially after a new trade route linked Cyrenaica with Wadai in the south. The Ottomans had a presence in the towns of Benghazi, al-Marj, and Darna, but their attempts to expand into the hinterland were rebuffed, especially after the rise of one of the most influential socioreligious orders in North Africa, the Sanusiyya.[35]

The Sanusiyya was founded by an urban religious scholar from Algeria, Muhammad bin Ali al-Sanusi (1787–1859), who began his movement in 1842 with the building of *zawayya* (lodges) in Cyrenaica. Selecting Cyrenaica because of its remoteness from colonial and Ottoman reach,[36] al-Sanusi based his order on trade, the complex regional tribal structure, and an ideology of revivalist Islam. The ideology integrated many ethnic and racial groups under its banner, resulting in the Sanusi order's proliferation throughout North Africa and the Sahara by the end of the nineteenth century.[37] A de facto state resting on an infrastructure composed of a network of lodges, the Sanusiyya replaced the Ottoman administration, providing education, security, and justice to the region.

CLASS FORMATION

By the time Italy seized Libya as a colony in 1911, new social classes had begun to emerge in Tripolitania. One class was composed of peasants (tribesmen) who had settled on small plots of land as sharecroppers. The second class included wage laborers from British and Italian companies. The third was a bourgeois class that was composed of urban notables who were either salaried bureaucrats or compradore merchants who traded with Europe.[38]

The emergence of these classes was not without conflict, especially among the bourgeoisie, whose urban notables jostled for land and administrative positions. The bourgeoisie also included new groups, such as urban intellectuals who became prominent during the reform period (1908–11) when newspapers began publishing, although new class divisions did not entirely eliminate tribal political alliances. The losers in the process of class formation were peasants and ordinary tribesmen who had little or no land yet had to pay taxes. Tripolitania had many small peasant communities, some of which, like the Amazigh Berber, adhered to Ibadi Khariji Islam.

The collapse of Fezzan's economy as a result of the dwindling of the Sahara trade led to the collapse of that region's class structure. Many merchants, peasants, and tribesmen faced impoverishment or migration—they chose to migrate. By 1911, Fezzan's population declined to 36,000 from 75,000, which was the population at the beginning of the 1800s.[39]

The Cyrenaican economy, conversely, was flourishing by the middle of the nineteenth century due to the new trade route joining Wadai, Darfour, Cyrenaica, Europe, and the Near East, and the strength of the Sanusiyya socioreligious movement. Sanusiyya lodges provided settlement, education, and economic networks for trade, linking Cyrenaica especially with Egyptian markets. The Sanusiyya also integrated tribal and intertribal alliances within the religious ideology of Islam, thereby avoiding the rivalries and fights among Tripolitanian notables over land and bureaucratic positions.

CONCLUSION

An understanding of the distinct regional economies of Tripolitania, Fezzan, and Cyrenaica, and their response to capitalist and military forces beyond their borders is essential to comprehending the diverse Libyan reactions to the Italian colonial conquest in 1911. Between 1835 and 1911, the second Ottoman state was engaged in a process of weakening or eliminating tribal chiefs, while they built a bureaucracy capable of ruling Tripolitania and Fezzan. Their political control over the Tripolitanian hinterland and Fezzan was enhanced by rural dependence on urban markets, and the fact that the city of Tripoli was not only the capital, but also the major market for trade and agricultural products. At the same time, however, competing peasant, tribal, and capitalist interests served to fragment the social structure of Tripolitania. The Ottoman's state-formation efforts failed to reach rural Cyrenaica, given the Sanusiyya's success in blocking Ottoman control. Far from encountering a strong, unified Libya in 1911, the Italians faced a sprawling country of diverse regions, tribal allegiances, and social forces.

2

THE REDISCOVERY OF THE STATE OF AWLAD MUHAMMAD: SOURCES AND SIGNIFICANCE, 1550–1813

[the] Awlad Muhammad Oh good heaven! If the means [of power] is snatched away from them. They fly away as a flock of pigeons. It scatters and returns again to the dispersed point.

A southern Libyan Fezzani folk song

The city of Tripoli was occupied in 1510 by Spain, as were parts of Algeria and Morocco. The Ottoman navy arrived on Tripoli's shore and took the city from the Knights of Saint John of Malta, who were allies of Spain in 1551. Tarabulus al-Gharb became an Ottoman province,[1] but Ottoman sovereignty did not penetrate the hinterland because of the desert ecology, the lack of revenues for a major cross-desert campaign, and the existence of another state—that of Awlad Muhammad, in Fezzan.[2] Beginning in 1560, the Ottoman state had to compete not only with armed tribal confederations but also with regional states such as the Awlad Muhammad in Fezzan (1550–1813) and the Sanusi state in Cyrenaica (1870–1911).

The ability of regional states and tribes to contest the power of the central state in Tripoli derived from an ecological distance from the central state, as well as from strong socioeconomic ties with other regional markets and tribes in neighboring countries. One must keep in mind that prior to the colonial period and the colonial conquest in 1911, strict borders were nonexistent, as were local ties to just one state. The tribes of western Tripolitania and southern Tunisia had strong confederations and were tied to the larger Muslim community of the Maghrib and the Sahara. The state of Awlad Muhammad in Fezzan was linked to the Lake Chad region for trade and the recruitment of soldiers. It also formed a strategic frontier refuge from the Ottoman state in time of war.

THE STATE OF AWLAD MUHAMMAD, 1550–1813

Sources: Primary and Secondary

The state of Awlad Muhammad was founded around 1550 by a Sharifian (one who claimed to descend from the prophet's family) from Fes in Morocco.[3] The descendants of Muhammad al-Fasi ruled the region of Fezzan and made alliances with other states in the region of Lake Chad. Fezzan's proximity to the Lake Chad region made it a strategic market for the many trade caravans. The market of Fezzan paved the way for the rise of local states. Many states had emerged along major trade routes in the Sahara and the rest of North Africa over the centuries, so the rise of a state in Fezzan was not an anomaly. In Fezzan, two local states emerged: the Ibadi Banu al-Khatab state in Ziwaila in the tenth century and the Awlad Muhammad state in Murzaq, which lasted from 1550 to 1813 (see Figure 2.1). A third attempt to build a state was made by the chief of Awlad Sulayman, 'Abd al-Jalil, who ruled the region from 1830 until 1842, when the Ottoman army killed him. This led to the flight of his tribal coalition into the Sahara frontiers in today's Chad. Fezzan was a station for the Sahara trade caravans. The state of Awlad Muhammad was a tributary state like the sixteenth-century Ottoman state in Tripoli; it was dominated, as analyzed in chapter 1, by the Awlad Muhammad family, tribal chiefs, and the merchants of Fezzan who needed secure routes, stations, and markets for their caravans.[4]

In 1994, new Arabic documents on the state of Awlad Muhammad were discovered by Libyan historian Habib Wadaa el-Hisnawi. This discovery is a major event in understanding this regional Saharan state. The documents shed new light on the trade, marriage, local alliances, and relations with the Ottoman state and Bilad al-Sudan.[5] This discovery should encourage scholars to search for more documents kept by families in southern and central Libya today, and by the Ottoman Archives in Istanbul. The new primary sources, in addition to the secondary

Figure 2.1 The old castle of Murzaq, capital of the state of Awlad Muhammad in Fezzan.

ones such as the accounts by the two local historians, Ibn Ghalbun and al-Ansari, those related by Western travelers, and those found in a manuscript by an unknown writer named Tarikh Fezzan (*The History of Fezzan*) provide scholars with new information about this forgotten Fezzani state.[6] From these sources, we do know that the Fezzani state existed on tributes in the form of taxes extracted from the caravans of the Sahara trade that passed through Fezzan, for whom, in exchange, the state provided protection, a market, and housing for merchants.

German traveler Friedrich Hornemann, who visited the region in 1789, wrote one of the earliest descriptions of the state. He observed that the state received tributes from trade caravans and raided oases and other states for spoils. Caravans from Cairo paid the equivalent of $6 to $8 for each camel load sold in the market in Murzaq, whereas caravans from Bornu and the Hausa lands paid two *mithqals* of gold for each slave they sold.[7]

Murzaq, the capital, was inhabited by merchants of different ethnic backgrounds—Arabs from the city of Tripoli, Sukana, Jalo, and Egypt; sub-Saharan blacks from Bornu and the Hausa lands; and Europeans. The Awlad Muhammad state, in exchange for tributes from the merchants, provided the security for a large market where these merchants could buy food, rent houses and camels, hire guides, and meet other merchants. In addition, the capital, Murzaq, had a fine craft industry; dyed cloth from Murzaq was sought after by the merchants of the Sahara trade.[8]

The Awlad Muhammad state was a trading state. It emerged as a station for organizing and protecting trade caravans; in exchange, trade merchants paid the state tributes for each camel load. Fezzan provided the state of Awlad Muhammad with the largest market in the Sahara trade among Bilad al-Sudan, the Maghrib, and Egypt. The richness of the Fezzani markets naturally lured the Ottoman administration in Tripoli to take over the trade; Ottoman governors in Tripoli began to send armies to Fezzan for the purpose of collecting tributes. Awlad Muhammad sultans resisted the Ottomans; whenever defeated, they would withdraw into Lake Chad's region to recruit soldiers, especially their allies—the rulers of Katsina, and return when the Ottoman army had left Fezzan.

UNDER THE SHADOW OF THE OTTOMAN EMPIRE
1551–1711

A compromise with the Ottoman army was arranged by the Ulama of Fezzan in 1639. This compromise gave the Awlad Muhammad state Ottoman recognition in exchange for paying a yearly tribute in gold and slaves.[9] The compromise ended when Sultan Najib M. Jhaym refused to pay the tribute in 1682. The Ottoman army attacked Murzaq, led by Murad al-Malti, who killed the sultan. His son, Sultan Muhammad al-Nasir, agreed to pay the tribute until 1689. Once again, Governor Muhammad Sha'ib al-Ain dispatched the Ottoman army. But al-Nasir defeated the army and did not pay tribute until 1715.[10] At that time, Ahmad al-Qaramanli took power and founded an autonomous state in Tripoli.

The rise of the Qaramanli autonomous state in Tripoli (1711–1835) was part of a larger phenomenon throughout the Ottoman Empire in which provisional governors and urban tax collectors ('*ayan*) paved the way for the rise of autonomous states in the eighteenth century. The Qaramanlis, for example, were members of the Cologhli class. As Turks themselves, they became a powerful group because of their ties to the Ottoman military aristocracy. They were land owners, military personnel, policemen, and members of a tax-exempt class.

In 1711 Cologhlis became the ruling class. Even so, the Qaramanlis kept some formal ties with the Porte, the Ottoman state in Istanbul. When Qaramanli pashas needed political protection from European states, they often requested an Ottoman decree, or a *firman*, from the Porte prior to the appointment of any new pasha. Aside from these formal ties, the Qaramanlis acted independently and often opposed imperial Porte policy, as in 1815 when Yusuf Pasha allied with France against Ottoman policy. The Qaramanlis, however, did not have enough resources to crush all tribal confederations, nor to eliminate the state of Awlad Muhammad. Most of their revenue came from the sea: their success in building a small but effective navy enabled them to receive *atawa* (taxes) or tributes from commercial ships, especially those from small European states. The tribes of the hinterland were armed and self-sufficient. A claim to land depended on the tribe's ability to defend the land against other tribes. As a defense strategy, regional tribal alliances were developed to counter state armies, foreign conquest, and war over land with other tribes.

IMPERIALISM, THE QARAMANLI STATE AND THE END OF THE STATE OF AWLAD MUHAMMAD, 1711–1813

The Qaramanli pashas, like Yusuf, followed two policies. The first was to incorporate strong chiefs by granting them the right to collect taxes in exchange for either a percentage or exemption, as in the cases of the Nuwair clan of the Mahamid in the western Tripoli family, the Haduth clan in Cyrenaica, and Saif al-Nasir of Awlad Sulayman in the 1820s. The second policy was to send the army and loyal tribes to punish rebellious tribes or states. This occurred against the Awlad Muhammad in 1715 and the Juwazi tribes in 1817.

The Qaramanli state's strength reached its peak during the reign of Yusuf Pasha Qaramanli from 1795 to 1832 as a result of an increase in *atawa* from the sea. These tributes allowed the pasha to expand state authority into the hinterland. After the decline of sea tributes following the war with the United States and the restrictions imposed by England and France, Yusuf Qaramanli shifted his trade policy to compensate for his losses. The Fulani's expansion in Lake Chad, under the leadership of 'Uthman B. Fudi, led to their domination of the Sahara trade. Yusuf Qaramanli directed his policy southward to compensate for his loss of sea tributes.

In 1815, European states signed the Treaty of Vienna— the beginning of the Qaramanli party's decline—which banned piracy and the slave trade. Yusuf Qaramanli did not modernize his state and army, nor did he broaden his elitist Cologhli-controlled state by appealing to the larger population; in spite of these misguided policies, he continued his extravagant lifestyle. He began to borrow money from European merchants. As state revenues declined, however, he could not pay back his debts. To make things worse for him, England and France restricted their payment of tribute to Tripoli in 1820.[11]

This European pressure led to a change in the policy of Yusuf Qaramanli. As sea tributes (*Atawa*) declined, he turned to agropastoral taxes and the Sahara trade tributes as alternative sources of surplus. After Tripoli's war with the United States, Qaramanli reoriented his policy toward the hinterland and the Sahara trade. He exempted strong tribal chiefs from taxes, as in the cases of the Nuir clan of the Mahamid, the Saif al-Nasir clan of Awlad Sulayman, and the Haduth of the Bra'sa. In exchange, these chiefs agreed to aid the state in collecting taxes and tributes. As for the Sahara trade, the pasha aimed to control it directly, which meant a change from his predecessors' policies of coexistence with the Awlad Muhammad. The pasha organized a large *mahalla*, or expedition, which destroyed the Fezzani state in 1813. Further, he sent two *mahallas* to Kanem in 1819 and 1827 to aid his ally, Shaykh Muhammad al-Amin al-Kanimi, the ruler of Kanem. This drastic new policy highlights the importance of analyzing the state of Awlad Muhammad, essentially a trading state in Fezzan connecting Lake Chad's region with North Africa. The state of Awlad Muhammad lasted for centuries and deserves further analysis.

When the Ottoman army conquered Tripoli in 1551, it targeted the rich Fezzan economy, which could provide tributes of dates, gold, and slaves. Further, the Ottoman state needed to ensure the flow of trade caravans to Tripoli City. Conflict was inevitable between a tributary empire and a regional state. Eventually, the Ottoman army was sent to Fezzan to demand a yearly tribute to the state in Tripoli. However, because the Ottoman state in Tripoli had only a small army between 1551 and 1711, a pattern persisted in its relations with the sultans of Awlad Muhammad: whenever the state in Tripoli weakened, the Awlad Muhammad refused to pay tributes. This in turn led to the retaliation of the Ottoman army, which tried to collect the tribute by force. The Awlad Muhammad sultans, whenever defeated, would retreat to their allies in the Sahara frontiers in Bornu and the Hausa lands; they would return after they gained strength by gathering recruits and after the Ottoman army departed. In 1639, Ibn Ghalbun described a truce that had been reached between the Ottoman army and the sultan of Awlad Muhammad. The sultan agreed to pay a yearly *jiziya*, or tribute, to the central government in Tripoli, comprising

> four thousand mithqals of gold; two thousand in gold dior or dust and . . . the remaining two thousands in slaves. Each male slave would cost 25 mithqals, the price of a slave girl would be

30 mithqals. The Awlad Muhammad would bear the expenses of the slaves until they reached Sukana. Beyond Sukana the expenses would be the responsibility of the government of Tripoli.[12]

The Ottoman commander, 'Uthaman Dey, recognized the state of Awlad Muhammad and gave the title of *shaykh* to Muhammad B. Jhaym. However, the tribute to Tripoli was irregular whenever the central state weakened; the Fezzani population supported Awlad Muhammad because of the brutality of the Ottoman army and its heavy taxation. Only after the rise of the Qaramanli state did the Awlad Muhammad pay tribute more regularly to the stronger Qaramanli state.

> When Hornemann visited Fezzan in 1789, he observed that the tribute to Tripoli was $6,000, reduced in the following year to $4,000. The state survived until 1812. Yusuf Qaramanli became heavily indebted to European merchants. To collect more revenues after the shrinking of the sea tributes, he shifted his policy southward toward the Sahara trade. Thus, the Awlad Muhammad became an obstacle to Qaramanli's new policy.[13]

Despite its military success in Fezzan, the Qaramanli state began to weaken as early as 1805. In that year the Pasha engaged in a war against the United States that ended in the restriction of his sea tributes. European pressure on North African states increased after the defeat of Napoleon in 1815 and consequent rise of British naval presence in the region.[14] The new conservative European alliance restricted piracy and vowed to punish the Barbary states, which included the Qaramanli in Tripoli.

The Sahara trade in the eighteenth century was based on the exchange of luxurious commodities such as cloth, guns, ostrich feathers, gold, goatskins, and slaves. European merchants wanted to export their cloth, guns, and luxury goods, and West African kings and aristocracies desired and could afford them. The local economy profited as well from engaging in this transit trade. The state protected trade caravans and received tributes. The local merchants made profits, and tribesmen from the Tuareg, Awald Sulayman, Zuwayya, and Majabra tribes served as guides, guards, and camel renters, while tribal chiefs received tributes from the merchants. By the turn of the nineteenth century, Tarabulus al-Gharb and the Sahara became markets for cheap British cloth sold at that time to the population at large, and not just to the elite. It should be noted that there was no separation between the means and the forces of production; tribesmen worked for wages for a season, and after that returned to their tribal land. In other words, free labor was not separated from communal and collective tribal identity—at least not until 1850.

Prior to the discovery of the Americas, gold and slaves were the most valuable commodities of the trans-Sahara trade. Indeed, West Africa provided Europe with most of its gold. Slaves were an equally important commodity before slavery was effectively banned in 1860. Slave trade across the Sahara became politicized as European states, especially England, legislated against it and started a campaign to ban it internationally at the turn of the nineteenth century.

CONCLUSION

Ottoman Libya was a regency removed from the central government, as well as a poor and marginal one when compared with those of other provinces such as Syria and Egypt. The regency was composed of many communities competing with the central state in Tripoli. Tribal confederations, as independent socioeconomic and political organizations, were able to compete with the weak states in Tripoli from the sixteenth century onward. The central government often had to compete with regional states, as in the case of the Awlad Muhammad state in Fezzan from 1550 to 1812. Merchants and peasants sought protection and security either from states or tribal confederations. Hence, the burden of *kharaj, jiziya,* and *atawa*—various kinds of tributes—fell mainly on peasants, slaves, client tribes, and merchants. Further, there was no single national state with complete control, nor was there only one market, but rather regions outside, like southern Tunisia, Bilad al-Sudan, and western Egypt. This was the general trend until the second half of the nineteenth century.

The discovery of the social history of the state of Awlad Muhammad contests the colonial and nationalist view of the Sahara as a space and a void between Bilad al Maghrib and Bilad al Sudan. The state of Awald Muhammad was Maghribian and African, and it had alliances in both the north and the Sahara. Thus it is time to question the colonial category of African studies divided into North Africa and sub-Saharan Africa, and to question the mythology of the modern nation-state as a category invented only in the last century.

3

FROM TRIBE TO CLASS: THE ORIGINS AND THE POLITICS OF RESISTANCE IN COLONIAL LIBYA

Fortunately for us, we come to know Italy had decided to occupy Tripoli, and my brother Salim and I joined with the Banco di Roma in denouncing publically the actions of the Young Turks committed against us. We offered them our cooperation in the occupation of the city of Tripoli.

Ahmad Diya al-Din al-Muntasar, Tripolitanian notable, 1919

Oh my homeland
You are twice ruined
All have left you
Some fled in exile
and others hung or murdered

Poet Fatima Uthman, 1929

My only illness is being at al-Agaila Camp,
the imprisonment of my tribe
and the long distance from home

Poet Rajab Hamad Buhwaish al-Minifi, 1930

INTRODUCTION

In early nineteenth-century Libya, townsmen, peasants, and tribesmen identified their interests according to kinship, regional, and religious ideologies rather than class affiliation. Although distinct classes existed, class formation was hindered by the self-sufficiency of seminomads and the peasantry, and the instability of the central state and private property. By 1911, when Italian rule of Libya began, the effects of eighty years of Ottoman state formation and the development of European capitalism had unsettled the old tributary social structure and fostered the emergence of more defined class configurations, which differed markedly among the country's three regions. Tripolitania had an urban notable class, peasantry, and tribal confederations, while Fezzan was dominated by tribal confederations, land-owning clans, and sharecropping peasants. Cyrenaica had no peasantry, and the formation of the Sanusi state integrated tribal factions into one cohesive social force.

These differing class configurations and the socioeconomic processes that produced them were largely ignored, not only by the Italian occupiers, but by several traditions of postwar scholarship. They perceived precolonial Maghrib society as an agglomeration of tribes or tribal states that were isolated from the larger social and economic structures of the region and modernized only under European colonialism.[1] This chapter calls such Eurocentric theories into question. I argue that the construction of a modern urban-centered state began in alliance with the Ottomans and suggest that under Italian colonialism, collaboration and resistance must be understood in reference to issues of state formation and political economy. Differing class configurations and degrees of socioeconomic development in Tripolitania, Fezzan, and Cyrenaica must be taken into account to make sense of the extent and type of collaboration and resistance among classes, tribes, and ethnic groups in Libya.

From 1835 on, when Ottoman rule began in Libya, Ottoman state formation proceeded through policies that curtailed the power of autonomous tribal chiefs and established an army, schools, courts, and postal and telegraph systems.[2] The Ottomans also recruited tribesmen and peasants from local populations for their police and army; by 1881 there were 12,000 troops in Tripoli City.[3] The abolition of tax exemptions and the institution of direct tax collection generated new revenues to support this state buildup. Yet many tribes refused to register their land, complicating tax collection.

Especially in Tripolitania, the strength of autonomous kinship ideologies also resisted and mediated Ottoman state formation for much of the nineteenth century. Kinship ideology was symbolized by the collective ownership of land. A belief in a common ancestor unified households, clans, and tribes, helping them to survive in a harsh, arid environment with limited water and pasture land. Kinship ideology applied not only to full members of these groups but also to clients, slaves, and artisans with lower status.

The self-sufficiency of a tribe encouraged identification primarily with that tribe and secondarily with that tribe's allies.[4] The most powerful tribal chiefs, Ghuma and 'Abd al-Jalil, refused to relinquish their status and autonomy, but the former was ambushed in 1842 and the latter was killed in 1858. Other chieftains reconciled with the state. As a general trend, seminomadism coexisted and allied with merchant capital,[5] and merchants allied with whoever gave them security. If the state could protect their trade, merchants would pay tribute to the state, but in the hinterland, merchants of the Sahara trade had to pay tribute to tribal chiefs to ensure free passage. Although private property existed in urban areas outside of the cities, in the hinterland collective tribal ownership still dominated.

CLASS FORMATION IN TRIPOLITANIA AND FEZZAN

The development of capitalism, which was fostered by Ottoman state reforms but also resulted from direct European capitalist intervention in the region, also acted to weaken the older tributary and pastoral economies. The decline of the Sahara trade devastated rural Tripolitania and especially Fezzan. Merchants were forced to return to their native towns;[6] British and Italian capital created job opportunities for tribesmen and peasants in urban Tripolitania as wage laborers in mills, construction sites, and on farms, as did French capital in the colonial territory of Tunisia.[7] By 1920 French Tunisia hosted over 20,000 Libyan immigrants, many of whom worked on olive tree plantations. The Ottoman state encouraged tribesmen still tied to the traditional pastoral economy to settle, tying them to its administration through incentives and taxes. After 1900, four classes emerged, all of which coexisted alongside the tribal confederation: a salaried 'ayan urban notable class, linked to the Ottoman state administration;[8] a compradore merchant class tied to British and Italian capital; a peasant class; and urban workers.

In Tripolitania, the decline of the Sahara trade and the development of capitalism facilitated new class formations through peasantization (settling tribesmen on the land) and proletarianization (the rise of wage laborers in towns).[9] Although class formations had existed during the first half of the nineteenth century, the instability of the central state and private property had meant that distinctions were not great. Now, the weakening of the major tribal confederation in the hinterland caused many tribesmen to lose their livelihoods as guides, renters of animals, and tribute recipients. Agriculture became the only major activity apart from herding. New peasants either worked their own plots of land through extended family labor or worked as sharecroppers for rich peasants and landlords. Other tribesmen worked as shepherds for rich tribal chiefs.[10] The Ottoman state encouraged settlement through land registration, security, a legal system that resolved disputes, and the introduction of new crops such as potatoes, cotton, coffee, and rice.[11] Through the payment of taxes, peasants became tied to the state administration and its courts. This peasantization was accompanied by small-scale proletarianization. Landless peasants and tribesmen moved to town and worked as wage laborers for British companies and Bank of Rome projects, or migrated to Tunisia (see Figure 3.1). This process of class formation was not necessarily deep, nor can it be viewed as replacing the old agropastoral and mercantile groups; rather, it ushered in changes such as increased urbanization, especially the development of Tripoli City as the larger urban market of the whole regency. By 1885, Tripoli had 20 bakeries, 22 mills, 1,109 shops, 40 wholesale stores, and 9 British and 11 Maltese firms, and Tripoli City's population went from 20,000 to 29,664 between 1883 and 1911.[12] Tripoli also began to exert a degree of hegemony over the countryside, providing political and economic services to peasants, tribesmen, artisans, and merchants of the hinterland. As Tripoli's courts, banks, schools, and markets gained in importance, urban institutions began to replace tribal institutions. The Tripolitanian regional economy was, thus, in transition from a communal and self-sufficient tributary trading economy to a mixture of tributary and capitalist economies. Capitalist penetration, while strong in coastal and eastern Tripolitania, did not affect seminomadic tribes, who continued to reproduce their tributary social relations.

Fezzan was much more affected by the decline of the Sahara trade, since its historic importance derived from its rich and strategic trans-Sahara trade markets. In Fezzan, a thriving date palm economy was the locus of transformations to settled agriculture. With around 1,175,000 palm trees, Fezzan also supplied most Libyans with dates, which were one of the country's basic foods. Yet by the turn of the century, social configurations revolving around Fezzan's rich trans-Sahara trade markets and a productive oasis agriculture had begun to give way to three distinct classes: (1) landowners (mostly Arab, Tuareg, Sharifian [the ones who claim kinship line with prophet Muhammad's family] and

Figure 3.1 A young rural girl and her brother in western Libya, 1963.

marabutic families [mystics who claim God's blessing]), (2) a small peasantry, and (3) sharecroppers. Tribesmen, the peasantry, and the urban poor paid the price for these changes through taxes, minimal wages, and the loss of tribal land.

The compradore merchant class benefited from the enhancement of Ottoman state authority and the transition to a more capitalistic economy, which meant greater communication and trading between cities and the hinterland. Composed mostly of Libyan Jews or Europeans (in large part Maltese, French, and Italian) and dominant in local and import-export trading, this group had its own courts, some tax exemptions, and state protection.[13] A number of these merchants, including Libyan Jews, held European citizenship and defended European interests before and during colonialism. In 1910, these non-Muslim traders and artisans numbered 18,093; these included 2,600 Maltese merchants who were British nationals, and 930 Jewish Libyan merchants who were Italian nationals. In the city of Tripoli alone, 8,609 Jewish Libyan artisans and traders had Ottoman nationality, and 500 others held French citizenship. Many other towns had Jewish merchants of foreign nationality: 40 Spanish Jewish merchants lived in Benghazi alone.[14]

The 'ayan, or Muslim bureaucratic notable class, also benefited from the strengthening of Ottoman authority. These notables acted as intermediaries between the Ottoman state and the local peasants, artisans, and tribesmen in matters such as revenue collection. Although they already represented the most educated and wealthiest segments of the population, the centralization of Ottoman power provided them with many new opportunities for advancement. Men from the Tripolitanian notable class (the 'ulama), the Cologhli (descendants of Turkish officers and local women), and the tribal elites provided the Ottoman state with authoritative religious interpreters, judges, court officials, teachers, and mosque shaykhs, filling most of the middle and lower administrative positions under the new system.[15] Although they increasingly fought over land and positions in the state bureaucracy, in the years preceding the Italian invasion of Libya—during the Young Turk rule (a Turkish nationalist movement that took power of the Ottoman Empire in 1908)—many of them found common ground in pan-Islamic ideology. This ideology did not replace tribal and religious affiliations but rather reflected the rise of an articulate urban class that would constitute one basis of resistance against the Italian occupiers.

CLASS FORMATION IN CYRENAICA

In Cyrenaica, the transformation of tribesmen into landlords, peasants, and wage laborers was the result of tribal wars, droughts, and state recruitment. This process occurred mainly within the regional economy of Cyrenaica (the western desert and the Nile Valley of Egypt) rather than inside Cyrenaica itself, since severe drought and intertribal war had forced some Cyrenaican tribes to migrate to Egypt starting in the eighteenth century. Exiled tribes fought over the best pastureland and water resources; throughout the nineteenth century and into the twentieth century, defeated tribes were pushed farther east into the Nile Valley, where they settled as peasants (*fellahin*). Understanding class formation requires that we look beyond colonial and nation-state boundaries, which are, after all, relatively recent and sometimes temporary creations.

In this region of Libya, the social and economic transformations that marked the years of Ottoman rule were shaped and managed by the Sanusi brotherhood. Originally a religious movement tied to anti-colonial resistance, the Sanusiyya grew by the early twentieth century into a de facto state that integrated both the elaborate Cyrenaica tribal system and the Sahara merchants. The Sanusi lodge system was crucial to the order's legitimation by both groups from the 1870s on. Because Sanusi lodges were located between tribal lands, they transcended tribal affiliations and served as stations for trade, cultivation, agriculture, worship, education, and the courts. Diverse ethnic and regional groups were unified under the banner of trade and Islam.

By the end of the nineteenth century, the Sanusi order had become deeply rooted as a state and as a religion: it organized trade, led prayers, and resolved disputes; it had territory, followers, and a judicial and bureaucratic structure. Thus it comes as no surprise that Sanusi followers voluntarily gave the Muslim *'ushr*, or tithe, to the Sanusi *shaykhs*, but refused to pay taxes to the Ottoman state. Indeed, since its inception, the order of the Grand Sanusi had aimed to educate its followers morally and socially to resist European colonial advances into northern and central Africa. As such advances intensified, so did both military training and education programs; students increased from 5,000 in 1897 to 15,000 in 1900.[16] Lodges provided such training for tribesmen, and the *zawiya* system at Jaghbub University offered weekly arms and equestrian instruction. By the time the Sanusi, under the leadership of Muhammed al-Mahdi, declared an official state in 1913 in response to the Italian occupation of Libya, the order had developed its own class structure, infrastructure, and ideology, and its lodges had effectively replaced the weak coastal towns of Cyrenaica as centers of economic, political, and civic life.

Sanusi social structure was by no means egalitarian. The dominant Sanusi family received a yearly tribute from their *waqf*, Islamic religious endowments land, which was exempted from Ottoman taxes. The brotherhood was dominated by two classes: the Ikhwan *'ulama* class of the Sanusi family and Sahara merchants. The elite *'ulama* class intermarried with the Sanusi family but not with members of other groups.[17] The Ikhwan and the merchants received most of the surpluses from trade and agropastoral products. The merchants profited from their investments in the Sahara trade, and the Ikhwan received yearly 'ushr alms, as well as *zakat*, or tributes in kind, such as wool, sheep, or grain.

The coming of European colonialism to the Sahara, which posed a threat to this power system, prompted a variety of responses. When the French expanded into Bilad al-Sudan (the "land of the blacks" in Arabic), which refers to the Sahara region from Sudan to Senegal, the Sanusi staged an armed resistance, fighting the French from 1897 to 1910 in what is now Chad. Yet they also demonstrated a pragmatic understanding of diplomacy, inviting the Ottomans to their territory in Cyrenaica in the wake of the French invasion in order to benefit from Ottoman diplomatic, legal, and military status. After a 1902 defeat by the French, for example, the head of the Sanusi order asked the Ottomans to send an official representative to its main center of Kufra as a sign of recogntion of Ottoman sovereignty over the Sanusi land, which prevented the French from invading there because they feared a clash with the Ottoman Empire.

The most serious danger, of course, came from the north, beginning with the Italian invasion of Libya in 1911. When the Ottoman Empire signed a peace treaty with Italy in 1912 and left Libya, it granted independence to the Libyans, giving the Sanussiya the opportunity to declare an independent state in 1913 with jihad (holy war) as its ideology. By 1916 the Sanusi family governed Cyrenaica and Fezzan and was able to mobilize a large army, which fought alongside the Ottomans against the British in western Egypt that year. Sanusi forces also offered the largest base of resistance against the Italians, and for twenty years Cyrenaica remained the center of Libyan opposition to colonial rule.

CLASS STRUCTURE AND COLLABORATION DURING ITALIAN OCCUPATION

In postcolonial Libyan historiography, collaboration with the Italian colonial state is poorly studied, in part because postindependence Libyan nationalism drew its stock of heroes, martyrs, and legends from the anticolonial resistance. History was used socially and politically by postcolonial states in both the monarchical years of 1951 to 1969 and the republican eras. Due to political censorship of national history by the state beginning in 1951, sources on collaboration, such as memoirs and other documents, are still guarded by concerned families; only after 1970 did new material become available to researchers as the new regime was eager to discredit the monarchical view of history. Postcolonial Libyan studies tend to reduce the motives of the *Mutalinin* (those who "went Italian") to a lack of moral character. Such reductionist views ignore the social backgrounds and the complexity of motives of Libyans who lived through the Italian occupation.

Indeed, reactions to colonialism took many complex forms, including armed resistance, trade, negotiation, invasions, emigration, accommodations, and collaboration. The reactions of various factions of Libyan society differed from one region to another as well as within each region. This diversity stemmed from the unequal socioeconomic development of each region in relation to urban markets and the degree of capitalist penetration. Whereas Tripolitania was partially penetrated by finance capital and portions of its hinterland became integrated into Tripoli City, the Sanusi order had a weak socioeconomic relationship with the coastal towns.

In Tripolitania, Italian colonial policy makers tried to buy off local notables and merchants as early as the 1890s. Local collaboration with the Italian state surfaced after 1918 as the Italians exploited competition among Tripolitanians with money, arms, and promises to appoint them as administrators. However, collaboration among old-class notables was not the dominant pattern in Tripolitania; most of Tripolitania's urban notables, especially those who were pro-Young Turks, emerged as the main leaders of the resistance.

Big compradore merchants, especially those tied to the Bank of Rome, sided with Italy to protect their economic interests. Collaborators of this class, such as Hassuna Qaramanli, the mayor of Tripoli (Figure 3.2), powerful Muslim merchants like the Muntasir clan, and Jewish merchants such as the Halfuns family, not only facilitated Italian economic and cultural interests in Tripoli City but even aided the Italian army in occupying the city.[18]

Through the Italian consulate in Tripoli, Mayor Hassuna was in contact with the Italian government from 1890 on.[19] His motive for collaborating with the Italians was his ambition to become the ruler of Tripoli like his grandfather, Ali Qaramanli. Believing the Italians would install him as ruler of Libya in the same way the French alliance had installed the local Hussaynid dynasty in Tunisia after 1881, he helped the Italian army by collecting Ottoman-distributed guns from the city on October 4, 1911.[20] However, the colonial authorities did not appoint him ruler as he had no influence outside the city, instead awarding him the vice governorship of the city.[21]

Another example of upper-class collaboration is found among the members of the Muntasir notable merchant class.[22] The Muntasir

Figure 3.2 Hassuna Pasha Qaramanli, mayor of Tripoli, 1911.

clan emerged as merchants in the coastal town of the Misrata during the second half of the nineteenth century, replacing their rival clan, the al-Adgham, after the defeat of the latter in the rebellion of 1835 to 1858. 'Uthman al-Adgham, the agha of Misrata, allied with the rebels against the Ottoman state.[23] By the end of the nineteenth century, 'Umar al-Muntasir and his sons became wealthy and rose to the top of the newly organized local bureaucracy. The wealth they accumulated from trade allowed them to build a clientage and intermarry with members of other prominent clans in the region.[24] These kin connections with other notables help explain why, until 1908, the Muntasirs were accepted locally by other notables as administrators of Gharyan, Tarhuna, Misrata, and Syrte.

In 1908 the Muntasir clan and other urban merchants and notables working for the well-paying Bank of Rome sided with Italy against the government of the Young Turks. Like most collaborators, the Muntasirs justified their actions as a defense against what they saw as harassment and a bias against their interests. As a merchant family, they wanted to retain their fortune and influence in the region. They were also motivated by a desire for revenge against their rivals in Tripolitania.[25] Ahmad Diya al-Din al-Muntasir was in Rome just before the invasion, consulting and advising the colonial officials on Libyan affairs. His father, 'Umar, used his influence to aid the army in occupying Tripolitania, Misrata, the city of Surt, and later Fezzan.[26] In exchange, the Italian colonial authorities kept them on as advisors and administrators.[27]

Jewish middlemen tied to Italian interests also welcomed and collaborated with the Italians prior to and during the occupation. Many merchants dominated the import-export trade with Italy and spoke Italian. When Italy began its policy of cultural and economic penetration, the Jews in Tripoli were eager to enroll in Italian schools, work for the Bank of Rome, and write for Italian newspapers. In 1907, the first Tripoli newspaper in a European language was the Italian *Eco di Tripoli*, edited by Gustavo Arbib.[28] In sum, economic interests motivated many merchants to collaborate with the colonial Italian state. Poor Jews were less enthusiastic than rich merchants; however, it seems that most Jews welcomed the Italians.[29]

There were also collaborators whom one could call *waverers*, the ones who waver between collaboration and resistance in the Tripolitanian interior. Tribes that still lived on the periphery and had been rivals of the Ottoman administration or that had been active in the resistance at other times, either did not view the Italian expansion into other areas as inimical or accepted Italian money and arms and fought on the side of the Italian army. These tribes saw their actions not as collaboration, but as a means of getting even with their rivals. Other tribal leaders fought the Italians until they were killed or forced into exile. The explanation of such diverse actions depends on the issue of tribal politics in late nineteenth-century Tripolitania.

A review of oral histories collected by the Libyan Studies Centre and my own interviews reveal a persistent trend: many notables and chiefs were eager to retain their administrative positions even after the Ottoman Empire signed a peace treaty with Italy in October 1912 and withdrew from Libya. These positions gave local notables access to state salaries, as well as the ability to offer favors to their kin groups by using their influence in the bureaucracy. As the Ottomans withdrew from Libya and local government emerged in Tripolitania, local notables began to make alliances, rewarding certain notables over others. These alliances affected some notables and chiefs who became bitter and wanted to get even, or preserve their influence with those who threatened and imperiled their power by excluding them from bureaucratic leadership. Some of these notables and chiefs joined the Italian side to correct what they saw as injustices committed against them. In short, the Italian army was not the main enemy; many chiefs regarded rival chiefs as more urgent threats to their status and power. Because many chiefs did not have religious or nationalist goals, they had no difficulty collaborating with the Italian state to protect their tribal or economic interests. Colonialism was, for these chiefs and notables, a pragmatic way to preserve their interests and positions.

Collaboration and factionalism among notables ultimately undermined the Tripolitanian resistance, which had 15,000 fighters in 1913.[30] Over the next years, Ottoman arms and money strengthened the power of those notables and chiefs who had decided to resist Italian occupation, and in 1918 Tripolitanian urban notables and rural leaders reconciled and formed the Tripolitanian Republic (1918–20), which, while unrecognized by Italian, French, and British governments, delayed the definitive Italian occupation of Tripolitania until 1923.

In Cyrenaica, too, urban notables collaborated with the Italian state. This was particularly true of the coastal urban areas, which had only weak ties with the Sanusi-dominated hinterland. Further isolated under Italian occupation, they became targets of fascist propaganda, and many notables accepted the jobs and salaries proffered them by the Italians. Years of education and mobilization by the Sanusi state had created cohesion among Cyrenaican tribes and an anticolonial mentality that fostered resistance by a volunteer army. Sanusi forces prevented Italian troops from expanding past the coastal areas, and between 1916 and 1922, Italian colonial policy shifted its course to make peace with the Sanusi. The 1916 Agreement of al-Zuwaytina recognized Italian sovereignty along the coast and Sanusi sovereignty in the hinterland, allowed for free trade, exempted Sanusi land and Zawayya from taxes, and granted the Sanusi family and the senior Ikhwan monthly salaries in exchange for disbandment and disarmament of Sanusi tribes.[31]

Some senior Sanusi tribal leaders refused to give up their arms, most notably Shaykh 'Umar al-Mukhtar, who was a veteran of the anticolonial wars against the French and British (Figure 3.3). These men, who came from lower-status tribal backgrounds, espoused pan-Islamic anticolonial ideology and became the protagonists of a protracted guerrilla war waged against the Italian fascist colonial armies between 1922 and

Figure 3.3 Shaykh 'Umar al-Mukhtar, charismatic leader of the eastern Libyan anticolonial resistance, 1931.

1932. In fact, this volunteer guerrilla resistance occasioned a social revolution inside Cyrenaica that pitted al-Mukhtar and other nonelite tribal commanders against a Sanusi leadership that had increasingly ceded to, and collaborated with, the Italians. Mass deportations to concentration camps and other genocidal practices by the fascists succeeded in ending the resistance but created martyr figures such as al-Mukhtar, who was executed at the age of sixty-nine in front of

20,000 Cyrenaican tribesmen and tribeswomen in 1931. Al-Mukhtar's story is covered in the next chapter.

CONCLUSION: COLLABORATION AND CLASS FORMATION

As in other peripheral societies, factionalism in Libya led to collaboration with oppressors. Each faction sought allies as the safest means to protect their authority and interests, especially in the context of colonial rule. Departure of the Ottoman army and bureaucrats after 1912 led to competition among notables over tax revenues and Ottoman and German aid, inhibiting the rise of unified leadership. Against this background, several types of collaboration emerged motivated by class interests, the political ambition of upper classes, and ethnic divisions of labor. Exploited by the Italians through money, arms, and promises of political appointments, collaboration led to the early crushing of the resistance and the 1923 occupation of Libya.

Reactions to colonialism took forms ranging from armed resistance, trade, negotiation, invasions, emigration, accommodation, and collaboration. The responses differed from one region to another as well as within regions depending upon socioeconomic development, availability of urban markets, and the degree of capitalist penetration. As early as the 1890s, the Italian colonial policy makers used the ambitions of local notables and merchants to create friction among classes, tribes, and ethnic groups. To understand resistance movements, we need to take a regional approach to examine why these different groups were led to cooperate with the colonial state as guides, soldiers, or informants.

As we have seen, these diverse regional socioeconomic changes that had occurred over the nineteenth century produced distinct classes in the three Libyan regions by the time the Italians occupied the country in 1911. Tripolitania had an urban notable class, a peasantry, and tribal confederations. Fezzan was dominated by tribal confederations, landowning clans, and sharecropping peasants. Cyrenaica had no peasantry and the Sanusi state had integrated tribal factions into one cohesive social force. In Tripolitania, precolonial, socioeconomic changes under the Ottoman modernization programs created negative differences among some social groups who were left out. Ottoman policies and Italian investment encouraged some groups to collaborate with the Italian colonial state for different motives. These polices affected collaboration with Italian colonialists and account for why these groups cooperated with the Italian state as guides, administrators, soldiers, and informants in the first decade of the occupation. In Fezzan, the Riyah and the Magarha tribes, who were rivals to the Awlad Sulay-man tribes before 1911, collaborated with the Italian state as a strategy to get even with their rivals. Such collaboration should be seen as an act of self-interest before the formation of modern Libyan nationalist ideology. Similar cases can be seen in other regions, as in the case of the Wurfalla and Mashashiyya tribes in eastern Tripolitania, but research needs to be done on the archival sources and family collections to discover the operation of the various groups that collaborated and to shed more light on the politics of collaboration as distinct from the idealized colonial sources and the condemnations of the nationalist school of Libyan history. This is why I turn now to the most ignored topic: the deportation and internment of half of the population of eastern Libya to brutal concentration camps, and how the victims of these camps preserved the memories of their experiences in their oral traditions, folk poetry, and memoirs.

4

ITALIAN FASCISM—BENIGN?
COLLECTIVE AMNESIA CONCERNING
COLONIAL LIBYA

Mussolini's Fascist dictatorship was a much more benign dictatorship than Saddam Hussein's.

Silvio Berlusconi, Italian Prime Minister

[Mussolini's fascism] up to 1938 was not totalitarian, but just an
ordinary nationalist dictatorship developed logically from a mul-
tiparty system.

Hannah Arendt, *The Origins of Totalitarianism*

Every day we counted about fifty dead bodies who were taken
from the concentration camp for burial. They were either hanged,
or shot by the guards, or died because of hunger and diseases.

**Salim 'Umran Abu Shabur, a survivor of the 'Agaila Colonial
Concentration Camp, 1929–1933, quoted by Eric Salerno in**
Genoicido in Libia

With the exception of a few courageous scholars, the genocide
(1929–33) of Libyan nationals at the hands of Italian fascists remains

virtually unknown to all but the Libyan people. The silence with respect to Libya on the part of most respected scholars of comparative fascism has contributed to a persisting notion that Italian fascism was somehow moderate or "benign." This chapter challenges the dominant historiographical view, which is based on the myth that Italian fascism did not encompass acts of genocide and mass murder and was therefore a lesser evil than the fascism practiced under the German Nazi regime. Secondly, it argues against the use of the nation-state and region as a unit of analysis. It is far more revealing, I believe, to use a comparative analysis that includes the European colonies in a global capitalist world system, especially after the eighteenth century.

I argue that one could not write the history of Italy without studying the history of its colonies, especially Libya. Similarly, one cannot write the history of Libya without studying the history of Italy. Both Italian and Libyan colonial and nationalist historiographies are limited if not distorted if the nation-state constitutes the unit of scholarly analysis. This chapter addresses three questions:

1. Why does the dominant image of Italian fascism as benign persist in the public media and scholarly studies when compared with Nazi Germany's model of fascism?
2. What are some of the moral and scholarly flaws of this myth of Italian fascism?
3. How does recovered evidence of Arab genocides between 1929 and 1933, along with oral narratives of some of the 100,000 victims of Italy's concentration camps in Libya, undermine common misconceptions concerning the nature of Italy's brand of fascism?

While none of these questions may be answered definitively here, the material presented in this chapter sheds light on the actual record of Italian fascism and could reorient current historiographic views. It is my main argument that Italian fascist brutality is not just a case of war accidents but rather genocide experienced by real human beings who are capable of telling us, in their own words and poems, about what they went through. This genocide has had a profound impact on today's society in Libya. My argument includes examples of public perceptions and scholarship; the context and causes for such views; alternative critical scholarship; the history of fascist genocide in Libya based on the agency and narrative of a Libyan who survived the concentration camps between 1929 and 1933; and suggestions for a new research agenda based on a critical model of Italian fascism.

EUROCENTRIC SCHOLARSHIP

Cultural stereotypes, as well as colonial and Eurocentric historiography, have contributed to the myth that Italian fascism was benign. Eurocentric scholarship ignores its policies in the colonies, while colonial scholarship views fascism as one component of the modernizing phase of history. Turning a blind eye to the nature of Italy's fascism is bolstered not only by official refusal to open the Italian National Archives to scholars, especially the files on its colony's concentration camps, but in the rejection of war crimes trials for individuals who carried out government policies as colonial officers. In addition, the Italian neo-fascist party has been waging a strong public relations campaign in defense of fascism since their reemergence in the body politic in early 1990.[1]

In 1972, Princeton University historian John Diggins published a comprehensive book on the official and popular images of Italian fascism in the United States. He argued that in the nineteenth century, Americans considered Italy, on one hand, to be a positive, romantic ideal, and on the other, a negative *nativist* country. Travelers and expatriate writers who viewed Italy as the classical source of cultural values shaped the romantic image and, in turn, shaped the perceptions of scholars focusing on national character and political culture. One must wonder whether cultural differences among the dead are worth mentioning. German Nazis killed Europeans, creating outrage among other Europeans, but Italian fascists killed North African Muslims, playing into orientalist fantasies, and colonial racist and modernist ideologies about the dehumanized, backward natives and the price of modernity. These perspectives created the context in which Italian fascism was seen as gentle—perhaps an aberration—while the German character, commonly viewed as militaristic, naturally resulted in the horrors of the Nazis.[2]

In the United States, the nativist image emanated from fear of Italian working-class immigrants, who were seen as ignorant, poor, and oppressed at the turn of the twentieth century. Even with the rise of fascism in 1922, American official and public responses to Italy were mostly positive, focusing mainly on Mussolini who, according to Diggins, represented a much needed solution to a country lacking discipline and work ethics and corrupted by a fractured elite. In the popular view, Mussolini, in fact, had multiple virtues. He was considered an accomplished writer, a violinist, a strong statesman, and a modernizer who "made the trains run on time." This image of Mussolini and his brand of fascism became popular in films and documentaries of the 1930s.[3]

One must keep in mind the larger historical context between 1922 and 1939. Italian fascism not only did not pose a threat to American interests, but the United States welcomed the anticommunist ideology of a country that had the largest communist party in western Europe. Even critics of Mussolini portrayed him merely as a buffoon or ordinary dictator.[4]

Movies played a major role in Mussolini's popularity. In 1931, Columbia Studio Company produced *Mussolini Speaks*, a film based on the dictator's tenth anniversary speech in Naples. It presents a positive view of Il Duce. In the 1920s, the Italian government opened its doors to the American film industry and tried to use films as a public relations tool.[5] This image of romantic Italy and a moderate Italian fascism still persists in the popular culture as shown in the 1999 film, *Tea with Mussolini*. This film claims to be more realistic. As a biographical film by the veteran Italian filmmaker Franco Zeffirelli, it dramatizes two aspects of Italy's colonialist era—British and American romantic images and the rise of anti-Semitism—through the lives of four expatriates and an Italian teenager (Zeffirelli as a young boy) in Florence in the late 1930s. Stanley Kauffmann astutely captured the significance of the film:

> Italy has long figured in the English imagination, especially writers. More of Shakespeare's plays take place in Italy than any country except England. But possibly it was the Brownings, Robert and Elizabeth, who set the still-prevailing affinity. When Elizabeth died in Florence in 1861, the municipality placed a tablet on her house with some lines by an Italian poet: "here wrote and died Elizabeth Barrett Browning . . . who made of her verse a golden ring linking Italy and England." Since that day a steady line of English residents in Florence has kept that ring polished. It is at Elizabeth's grave that *Tea with Mussolini* begins.[6]

The movie is silent about the colonial fascist atrocities in Libya despite the fact that these atrocities happened earlier between 1929 and 1934.

Today there are still scholars who advance the notion of moderate Italian fascism and Mussolini's value. The contemporary rise of the Fascist Party in Italy, the New Alliance, lends credence to the theory that Italian fascism helped modernize Italy, especially after it captured 14 percent of the vote or 100 of the 630 seats in the Italian lower house and joined the government as a legitimate party in 1994. In 2001 Gianfranco Fini, the head of the party, became deputy prime minister in Mr. Berlusconi's government, and on November 20, 2004, he became the new Italian foreign minister. The *New York Times* described him as a reformed leader who denounced anti-Semitism and visited Israel twice.[7] Denouncing Jewish anti-Semitism is a positive development, but what about the other Semites, the Libyan Muslims who experienced fascist atrocities? The new party used one of its most charming members, Mussolini's granddaughter Allesandra, to display to the American public. Her pictures in *People* magazine (April 29, 1992) are revealing. In one, Allesandra Mussolini raises her arm in the fascist salute, just as her grandfather Benito did on a balcony in the eastern Libyan city of Benghazi. The article in *People* identified the place but misspelled Benghazi as *Bangali* and did not identify it as part of Italy's colonial holdings.[8]

Young Allesandra Mussolini represents the far right Italian Social Movement (Movement Sociale Italiano or MSI). She seems an industrious modern woman who promises to show people what a Mussolini can do. Her grandfather's followers founded the MSI in 1946, but it has been a marginal force until recently when it became a partner in the coalition government of Silvio Berlusconi. Fascism is becoming respectable again, not because it is less evil, but because we have forgotten what it means.

Advocates of the myth that Italian fascism was moderate in comparison to Germany's base their case on two arguments: (1) that the Italian approach to anti-Semitism was milder, and (2) that there were no mass killings or ethnic genocide such as that carried out by Nazi Germany. Here the scholarship on fascism tends to focus on the regime's treatment of the European Jewish minorities. This thesis is supported with information such as the fact that the Fascist Party was open to Jews, and that more than twenty Jews joined a Fascist Party march on Rome in 1922. Further, high-ranking officials in the fascist state included Italian Jews such as Aldo Finzi, a member of the first fascist council; Guido Jung, minister of finance from 1932 to 1935; and Maurizio Rava, governor of Italian Somaliland and a general in the fascist militia. Philosopher Hannah Arendt, who wrote the most influential book on the origins of totalitarian regimes in the last century, argued that there was no Jewish question in Italy, and that only after pressure from the German Nazi state did Italy turn in seven thousand Italian Jews to the German concentration camps. For her, Italian fascism is just an ordinary dictatorship. Her Eurocentric approach to Italian fascism has contributed to the persistent myth that Italian fascism is a lesser evil and even moderate.[9]

On the other hand, Victoria de Grazia points out that "racial laws of 1938 modeled on Germany's 1935 Nuremberg Laws forbade interracial marriages between Italians and Jews, banned 'Aryan' servants from working in Jewish houses, removed Jews from influential positions in government, education, and banking."[10] A scholar of comparative fascism, de Grazia focuses her attention on Europe, therefore concluding that the Holocaust was unique in its mass killing of Jewish and other ethnic minorities. Her perspective, while critical of the prevailing scholarship in some respects, is like others shaped by a European approach.

ALTERNATIVE SCHOLARSHIP

Antonio Gramsci and postcolonial intellectuals such as Aime Ceasaire, Franz Fanon, and political economist Samir Amin have challenged Eurocentric interpretations of history, arguing that colonialism and the history of colonized peoples must be acknowledged.[11] Gramsci was aware of and critical of the brutal fascist colonial wars, despite the fact that he was locked up in the fascist prison most of his adult life.[12] In his famous book, *The Wretched of the Earth* (1961), Fanon contended, "Nazism turned the whole of Europe into a veritable colony."[13] The Africanist scholar Mahmood Mamdani has eloquently contexualized the debate about fascism, colonialism, and genocide: "The Holocaust was born at the meeting point of two traditions that marked modern Western Civilization: 'the anti-Semitic tradition and the tradition of genocide of colonized people.' The difference in the fate of the Jewish people was that they were to be exterminated as a whole. In that, they were unique—but only in Europe."[14] If one believes as a moral principle that all people, regardless of origin, count, and have the same intrinsic worth, then all acts of genocide must be recognized and all victims counted.

Ten years ago when I wrote my book on the making of modern Libya, I discovered that most scholars of fascism and totalitarianism viewed Italian fascism as a lesser evil. Because my studies—based on archival research and oral interviews with the elderly Libyans who fought Italian colonialism—confirmed its outrages, I was discouraged about this appalling case of historical amnesia.[15] Five years ago I began to collect primary material on fascist concentration camps in Libya, recognizing there are indeed some scholars and at least one journalist who are pioneers in the study of the history of genocide in Libya: E. E. Evans-Pritchard, Giorgio Roshat, Angelo Del Boca, Eric Salerno (journalist), Nicola Labanca, Ruth Ben Ghait, and Yusuf Salim al-Barghathi.[16] Despite differences in age, background, method and field of expertise, this group shares a focus on Italian fascist atrocities in Libya, especially concerning the concentration camps between 1929 and 1934.

Three historians stand out for their work in this area: Giorgio Roshat, Yusuf Salim al Barghathi, and Ruth Ben Ghait. Roshat, the main Italian historian courageously challenging official views, has searched colonial records on genocide in the concentration camps since the early 1970s. Al-Barghathi, a collector of oral interviews with Libyan camp survivors, wrote a major book based on these personal histories. Ben Ghait, a historian of Italian fascism, recently published an engaging and critical theoretical study of the notion of Italian fascism as a lesser evil.[17] These scholars offer a comparative perspective that brings the Libyan experience into the larger study of Italian fascism, and have been able to debunk the myth that Italian fascism was moderate.

THE LIBYAN RESISTANCE

In 1922 the Italian Fascist Party assumed power in Rome. As a component of their policies, they rejected the colonial practice (followed since 1911) of collaborating with local Libyan elites, terming it a failure. The fascists advocated military force aimed at "pacifying" the natives of Italy's colonies. Like apartheid in South Africa and Aryan supremacy in Nazi Germany, the Italian fascist policy was based on an ideology of racial supremacy. It stressed hierarchy, holding that as a superior race, Italians had a duty to colonize inferior races, which included, in their view, Africans. It was Mussolini's plan to settle between ten and fifteen million Italians in Eritrea, Somalia, and Libya to populate what he heralded as "the Second Roman Empire."

Fascist colonial policy meant forced subjugation of Libyans. Rights accepted before 1922 by the previous government were dismissed. Educational policies changed in accordance with racial supremacy views: while previous colonial officials had moved to "Italianize" Libyans by broadening education, the fascists barred Italian culture from natives, replaced the Italian language with Arabic in the classroom, and banned education to Libyans after the sixth grade. Beyond sixth grade, Libyans could work only as laborers.

Mussolini gave the task of *pacification* of Libya to the architect of the reoccupation of Tripolitania and the western and southern regions of Fezzan, the brutal General Rodolfo Graziani. While he had been successful elsewhere, Graziani discovered that Cyrenaica, the eastern region of Libya, posed the toughest challenge to Italian conquest of Libya. The general faced a cohesive force of Cyrenaican tribesmen and merchants forged from seventy years of education and mobilization by the Sanusiyya religious/social movement. Through their efforts, the Sanusiyya had brought together numerous tribes in an economically viable and culturally unified state. Under the Sanusiyya, taxes were levied on grain and animals (*'ushr*), and on the trans-Sahara trade—all caravans crossing Cyrenaica to trade with Egypt. Importantly, the people of the eastern region shared an anticolonial, pan-Islamic ideology. These economic and cultural forces cemented a unity in the eastern region that allowed Cyrenaican tribesmen to successfully resist Italian colonialism until 1932.

The volunteer-based native resistance movement confronting General Rodolfo Graziani was led by a legendary, charismatic, sixty-nine-year-old leader, 'Umar al-Mukhtar. The resistance's well-mobilized population included networks of spies even inside Italian-controlled towns. Graziani estimated the native guerrillas numbered around 3,000, and the number of guns owned by Cyrenaican tribesmen to be about 20,000. Unlike the Italian invaders, the Cyrenaicans were familiar with the geography of the Green Mountain valleys, caves, and trails. In 1931 alone, the guerrillas engaged in 250 attacks on, and ambushes of, the Italian army. Colonial Italian officials attempted first to bribe 'Umar al-Mukhtar, offering him a good salary and retirement. When he rejected the overture, Graziani moved to crush the resistance. The general's armies adopted a scorched-earth policy. This was compounded by cutting off the guerrillas' supplies with the construction of a 300-kilometer fence along the Libyan–Egyptian border, and then organizing a campaign to occupy Kufra, capital of the Sanusi order, deep in the desert. Graziani's army, including 20 airplanes and 5,000 camels, encountered fierce resistance by the Zuwayya tribe, but he succeeded in occupying Kufra on February 20, 1931 (see Figure 4.1).[18]

The success of the Cyrenaicans in withstanding General Graziani's assaults forms the context for understanding why Mussolini ordered Pietro Badoglio, the colonial governor of Libya, and General Graziani to quell the resistance by any means necessary. The archival records show that the fascist state's strategy was clear concerning the destruction of the resistance, even if it meant killing the civilian social base of the resistance. They responded by forcefully rounding up two-thirds of the civilian population of eastern Libya—an estimated 110,832 men, women, and children—and deporting them by sea and on foot to camps during the harsh winter of 1929. The deportation of the population emptied rural Cyrenaica and effectively cut off the resistance from its social base. Isolated on all sides and lacking supplies, the rebels gave up, especially after the capture and hanging of their leader, 'Umar al-Mukhtar, on September 12, 1931, and the arrest and killing of most of his aides on September 24, 1932.[19]

Figure 4.1   The capture of Shaykh 'Umar al-Mukhtar, 1931.

THE CONCENTRATION CAMPS

The policies of Italy's fascist government were unprecedented in the history of African colonialism, but it was not until recently that Western scholarship acknowledged forceful deportation of the rural population of Cyrenaica and their confinement in concentration camps between 1929 and 1934. Historian Giorgio Roshat discovered evidence that the Italians were prepared for large-scale civilian deaths in a letter written from Governor Badaglio to General Graziani in June 20, 1930: "We must, above all, create a large and well-defined territorial gap between the rebels and the subject population. I do not conceal from myself the significance and the gravity of this action which may well spell the ruin of the so-called subject population."[20]

The colonial state spent thirteen million Italian liras on the construction of the camps. Double barbed wire fences surrounded them, food was rationed, and the pastureland was reduced and patrolled. In the biggest camp, no one was allowed outside except by restricted permit. Forced labor was common, and no serious medical aid was provided. Outside the camp, Graziani ordered the confiscation of all livestock. Sixteen camps were constructed varying in size and degree of brutality from the encircled camps (al-Shabardag) outside the towns such as Diriyyana, Susa, al Marj, al-Abyar, Benghazi, Sidi Khalifa

Suawni al Taryia, al-Nufiliyya, Kuafiyya, and Ijdabiya, to the largest and harshest camps of Slug, Sidi Ahmad al-Magrun, and the Braiga. The terrible punishment camp al-Agaila was especially constructed for relatives of the rebel *Mujahidin*.[21]

For an independent seminomadic population, conditions were devastating. As usual, the sick, elderly, and children were the most vulnerable victims of these conditions, especially because the death of most of the herds ensured the people's death by slow starvation. British anthropologist E. E. Evans-Pritchard, an expert on the tribes of Cyrenaica, wrote,

> In this bleak country were herded in the smallest camps possible, 80,000 men, women, and children, and 600,000 beasts, in the summer of 1930. Hunger, disease, and broken hearts took heavy toll of the imprisoned population. Bedouins die in a cage. Loss of livestock was also great, for the beasts had insufficient grazing near the camps on which to support life, and the herds, already decimated in the fighting are almost wiped out by the camps.[22]

With colonial archives still restricted, there is little documentation of daily life inside the camps except for the oral history of the few Libyans who survived. Most scholars, including Evans-Pritchard, Roshat, Del Boca, and Labanca, agree that the camps decimated the population. Roshat summed up his research of Italian sources as follows: "The fall in population must be in small part attributed to war operations and, to a greater extent, to the conditions created by the Italian repression (hunger, poverty, and epidemics) and to the deportation of the people (transfer marches, death through malnutrition in the camps, epidemics, and inability to adapt to terrible new conditions)."[23] All agree that at least 40,000 people died in the camps due to shootings, hangings, disease, or starvation, but Libyan historian al-Barghathi places the death toll higher, between 50,000 and 70,000. His estimate is based on Libyan archives and oral interviews. He proved that the total number of the deportees is 110,832, which is much higher than previous estimates by Pritchard (80,000) and Roshat (100,000).[24] Yet Del Boca notes a fact ignored by most historians: large numbers of elderly adults and children died during the deportation from the Marmarika and the Butnan in the Green Mountain region in eastern Libya to the desert of Syrte in a grueling forced walk of 657 miles. The total death toll including the forced deportation, hunger, and diseases at the camp was at least 60,000. Roshat estimates that 90 to 95 percent of the sheep, goats, and horses, and possibly 80 percent of the cattle and camels died by 1934.

The destruction of the herds contributed to famine and death among the seminomadic population.[25]

This was not the first time that Italy deported Libyans since taking over the country as a colony in 1911. Between 1911 and 1928, as many as 1,500 Libyans sympathetic to the anticolonial resistance were exiled to Italian islands. The entire population of the oasis Hun in central Libya was deported to the coastal towns of Misurata and Khums in the aftermath of the battle of 'Afiyya on October 31, 1928. However, the massive deportation of the majority of Cyrenaica's population was unprecedented. The agony suffered in the camps along with the enduring loss of dignity and autonomy has left deep psychological scars on Libya's national memory.[26] Their colonial experience is unmatched, except perhaps for that in Algeria and the Belgian Congo. Observers should note that the Libyan people's first major encounter with the West was as a colony under an Italian fascist government. The fact that their experience, which includes exposure to genocide, has not been well studied or acknowledged and that no military or civilian colonial officials have been brought to trial have not helped to heal the scars of history (see Figure 4.2).[27]

In 1998 the Italian government made a joint public statement with the Libyan government acknowledging some responsibility of the Italian

Figure 4.2 Italian Fascist concentration camps, desert of Syrte, Libya, 1930.

atrocities in Libya during the colonial period between 1911 and 1943.[28] While such an announcement is welcomed, this vague and general statement falls short of facing the unresolved brutal history of genocide in colonial Libya. Italian fascism committed crimes inside and outside of Italy. Libya is the most brutal case, but people from Yugoslavia, Ethiopia, and Greece also experienced fascist oppression and internment. Full disclosure of the fascist archives must follow the recent positive official Italian admission of some responsibility about what happened in Libya. Only then can one talk historical truth and reconciliation.

RECOVERING THE ORAL HISTORY OF THE GENOCIDE: THE LEGACY OF FOLK POETRY

The statistical records of the genocide are very horrific, and what is more significant, but missing from current scholarship is the way millions of Libyans have interpreted the memory of this genocide. During the last five years, I have searched for records of the people who experienced deportation or the concentration camps. Had they left diaries? Memoirs? Were the people still alive, and if so, how could I find them? I found only a few published memoirs, but thanks to the Center of Libyan Studies in Tripoli, many survivors of the camps were interviewed for a published collection called *The Oral History of the Jihad*. Since most Libyans during the colonial period were illiterate and relied on memory as a counter to the official state history, it is no exaggeration to state that some elders are walking libraries.[29] The main source of historical views and Libyan culture has been folk poetry. This should not be a surprise; oral traditions and poetry are highly valued in Libyan rural culture, as most people were illiterate during the first half of the last century.[30]

I was aware of the significance of poetry to moral and cultural beliefs, but it was only after reading the collected books of Libyan folk poetry written during the colonial period that I realized it may offer by far the richest and the most illustrative source of Libyan colonial history, especially of the camp incarceration years of 1929 through 1934. Among the most notable are published memoirs by Ibrahim al-'Arabi al-Ghmari; al-Maimuni, who writes about his life in the Agaila (the most notorious concentration camp); and Saad Muhammad Abu Sha'ala, who also writes on life inside the camps. These provide powerful testimony, along with works by the most outstanding poet of the period, Rajab Hamad Buhwaish al-Minifi, who was interned in the Agaila camp and wrote the famous epic poem "Ma Bi Marad" (I have no ill except al-Agaila concentration camp). Known by most Libyans, the poem is a brilliant and damning reaction to the horrors of the camp and the impact of killing and suffering on freedom-loving semi-nomads. To my delight, I also discovered female poets, such as Fatima 'Uthamn from Hun, who composed the poem "Kharabin Ya Watan" (My homeland ruined twice) and Um al-Khair Muhammad Abdaldim, who was interned in the Braiga camp.[31] These poets offer powerful testimonies concerning the views of the men and women who experienced uprooting, exile, and displacement. They suggest that what they faced was a religious war and an ethnic cleansing.

The following summary is a new and original reconstruction of the history of the deportation and the concentration camps through the eyes of Libyan people, who experienced them firsthand. The narratives focus on themes of the deportation experience, daily life in the camps, food, clothes, forced labor, hunger, disease, punishment, depression, death, mourning, and struggle for survival.

The forced walk, or shipping of people and their herds from rural Cyrenaica, extended from Derna in the east to camps in the desolate desert of Syrte in northern central Libya. Tahir al- Zawi, a Libyan historian of that period, described the deportation of the people of Cyrenaica as the Day of Judgment described in the Quran.[32] Al-Ghmari al Maimuni writes,

We were forced in a ship in Benghazi without much food, and our women and children were crying and wailing. It was a very cold winter and many of the children and women passed out. When we arrived at the Agaila, the wind was so strong that we could not get off and we had to sail to an island nearby. The following day we landed; the ship was so filthy due to seasickness.[33]

Salim Muftah Burwag al-Shilwi was only thirteen years old when his family was deported from Darna by ship to Benghazi, and then to Zuwaitina. He wrote,

As we arrived in Zuwaitina, the guards began to shove us to the shore. The hated military commander Col. Barilla of the Agaila camp gave a speech addressing the deportees: "You Ubaidat tribe will be interned in the camps of Agaila and al-Braiga where you will die so we will have a stable Italian rule in Libya." Then he walked toward a young Libyan woman and touched her cheek and said, "Your cheek is white right now but very soon it will be as black as a black servant's".[34]

These autobiographical documents and oral history indicate that the aim of the fascist policy is the destruction of the culture and not just the individuals.

DAILY LIFE IN THE CAMPS

The guards for the camps were Italian colonial soldiers from Eritrea and Libya. Eritrean 'Askaris were Italian subjects who were recruited to serve as a cheap military labor in Libya beginning with the conquest in 1911. Also by 1929 the Italian colonial state found some Libyan collaborators who worked as guides, guards, spies, advisors, and soldiers.[35] They restricted daily life of their civilian prisoners to cleaning, loading and unloading goods, collecting wood, forced labor on major projects, and taking care of the ill and the dead. All of the interned had to salute the Italian flag and witness the execution of those accused of collaborating in any way with the anticolonial resistance. Any hint of disapproval or failure to salute the commander or Italian flag meant verbal abuse and physical punishment by whipping and confinement. The poet Um al-Khair described the guards as kinsmen of the devil.[36] Salim al-Shilwi recounts a time in the Agaila camp when a man who failed to salute the commander was whipped one hundred times. Then, when he refused to say, "Long live the king of Italy," he was whipped seven hundred more times.[37]

FOOD AND CLOTHES

Food was scarce. Survivors recount that they occasionally received rice but mainly subsisted on a pound of poor-quality barley doled out each week. With the confiscation or death of their herds, the interned suffered malnutrition and death. "Many of us in the Agaila camp ate grass, mice, and insects [while] others searched for grain in animals dung to stay alive," said Salim al Shilwi.[38]

Ali Muhammad Sa'ad al-'Ibidi noted, "At one time we counted about 150 deaths (mostly elderly and children) and the cemetery shows the evidence."[39] Muhammad Muftah 'Uthman said the tribe of 'Abaddla alone lost five hundred people to starvation.[40]

Without means of buying clothes, many of the interned were forced to wear the same clothes they had worn for three years. Their garments became rags—a further humiliation to rural women who value their modesty in dress.[41] Poet Muhammad Yasin Dawi al-Maghribi captured this loss of dignity in his poem "I saw a Shaykh," in which he describes the status of a well-dressed and respected elderly chief who ended up in the camp with dirty torn clothes, and how his degradation was reflected in his face and body language.[42] One survivor of the camps said that in the few cases where men and women got married, the dowry was a quarter pound of sugar.[43]

Poet Rajab al-Minifi captures this humiliation and the harshness toward women, whom courageous Bedouin men are supposed to protect:

I have nothing except the dangers of the roadwork
my bare existence,
returning home without a morsel to move down a gullet.

whips lash us before our women's eyes,
rendering us useless, degraded,
not even a matchstick among us to light a wick

nothing ails me except the beating of women,
their skins bared,
no hour leaves them undisturbed,

not a day without slander heaped on our noble women,
calling them sluts,
and other foulness that spoils a well-bred ear

I have no illness except the hearing of abuse,
denial of pleas,
and the loss of those who were once eminent,

and women laid down naked, stripped
for the least of causes,
trampled and ravished, acts that no words deign describe.

I have no illness except about the saying of "Beat them,
No pardon,"
and "With the sword extract their labor,"

the company of people unfamiliar to us,
a low life indeed
Except for God's help, my hands are stripped of their cunning.

I have no illness except the suppression of hardship and disease,
worry over horses …
and work for meager wages as the whips cry out lashing.

What a wretched life,
and when they're done with men, they turn on the women.[44]

FORCED LABOR

Forced labor was another aspect of concentration camp life. The interned Libyans were compelled to work on construction of a fence between Libya and Egypt, and on paving a new coastal highway between Syrte and Benghazi. Punishment, hunger, the lack of good hygiene, and minimal medical assistance combined to spread disease and eventually led to high death rates. Some people went mad and others fell into depression.[45] The poet Um al-Khair asked God to end this suffering for the Muslims and either let them die or help them defeat the Italian colonialists. While most prisoners eventually died in the camps from hunger and disease, those who survived carried with them the loss of human dignity and autonomy, mourning and sorrow.[46]

Poet Rajab Hamad Buhwaish al-Minifi, who survived the Agaila concentration camp, expressed this loss of dignity and autonomy probably more eloquently than any other poet in colonial Libya. His epic poem "Dar al-Agaila" (Under Such Conditions) deserves translation and special attention. He belonged to the same tribe as the leader of the resistance, 'Umar al-Mukhtar, and to understand his poem one should keep in mind his background. He belonged to a tribe that was autonomous prior to the Italian conquest in 1911. He does not talk about individualism and personal salvation but reacts as a member of a collective kinship community that values chivalry, freedom, generosity, dignity, and the open space of nomadic life. Al-Minifi belonged to a culture that developed a system in opposition to collaboration that thrived under the Sanusiyya social movement for a long time prior to and after the colonial conquest of Libya. He was also an educated man, a religious teacher who was educated in the Sanusi *zawayya* and the higher Institute at Jaghbub.[47] He starts his poem by stating that he is not ill except for the illness of living in Agaila and its impact, especially the loss of beloved kinsmen and women:

I have no illness except this endless aging,
loss of sense and dignity,
and the loss of good people, who were my treasure,

Yunes who rivals al-Hilali,
throne of the tribe,
Mihimmad and 'Abdulkarim al-Ezaila,

and Buhssain, his sweet countenance and open hand,
and al-Oud and the likes of him,
lost now without farewell to burden our day.

I have no illness except the loss of young men,
masters of tribes,
picked out like date fruit in daylight,

who stood firm-chested against scoundrels,
the blossoms of our households,
whose honor will shine despite what the ill-tongued say?

I have no illness except the absence of my thought,
my scandalized pride,
and the loss of Khiyua Mattari's sons,

Moussa and Jibril, sweet companions of night dirges,
masters of horses, tamers of wild camels,
unharmed by rumors calling them cowardly, meek.

I have no illness except . . .
being imprisoned by scoundrels,
and the lack of a cohort to complain to when wronged,

the lack of those who rule with fairness,
evenness nonexistent,
evil leaning hard on good, dominant.

I have no illness except my daughters that serve in despicable labor,
the lack of peace
loss of friends death has taken.

the capture of Al-Atati, azir al nussi,
Aiyez as well,
who soothes the heart in forlorn desiccated hours.

I have not illness except the loss of my herds,
and I'm not counting,
even while the taker has no remorse, no pangs of guilt

They bring nothing except rule by torture
and the long. . . .
and the tongue rived and sharpened with pounding abuse.

I have not illness except the lack of defenders,
the softness of my words
the humiliation of the noble-named,

the loss of my gazelle-like unbridled,
swift-limbed,
fine-featured like a minted coin of gold.

No strength, will, or effort to lift these burdens.
Of our lives we're ready
to absolve ourselves lest death's agent come.

Nothing ails me except the bad turn of my stars,
the theft of my property,
the tightness and misery of where I lie down to rest.

The fearsome horseman who on days of fray
shielded his women folk
Now begs, straggling after a tailless monkey.

Every day I rise complaining of subjugation,
my spirit disgraced,
and like a woman I can't break my chains.

I have no illness except the bent shape of my life,
my limpid, wilted tongue.
I would not tolerate shame and now shame has overtaken me.

At the end of the poem, the poet asks God for solace:

Only God is eternal. The guardian of Mjamam is gone.
The oppressor's light
Has befallen us, stubborn, unrelenting

If not for the danger, I would say what I feel,
raise him noble,
expound my praise of him, sound the gratitude we owe.

This epic poem suggests, more than any other poem, the trials of internment and displacement, illness, and enduring suffering as a theme across many poems. This poem strikes the reader as a significant alternative to death—"final solution"—a spirit of resistance and anguish.

The only rival to al-Minifi's brilliant poem is Fatima 'Uthamn's poem "Kharabin Ya Watan" (My homeland ruined twice), which she composed after she saw nineteen men hung by the Italian army in her home town, Hun, as punishment for supporting the anticolonial resistance in 1929. The rest of the people in her town were deported to the northern coastal towns of Misurata and Khums.

A PERSONAL STATEMENT

I would like to acknowledge a personal connection with the genocide in the concentration camps and the larger view of the victims of Italian colonialism in general. My Libyan grandparents lived through that colonial period and my parents witnessed its last phase in the 1940s. My grandfather's teenage years were spent as a freedom fighter in the anticolonial resistance, and my grandmother died in exile—away from her homeland—in Chad before I was born. When I came to the United States as a graduate student, I brought with me my family's anguish at their displacement and struggle for survival and love for oral history and poetry. When I was in college at Cairo University, I published poems in Libya for three years in the literary sections of the leading Libyan newspapers, the *Cultural Weekly* and the *New Dawn*. In the United States as a teacher and political scientist/historian, I have worked to tell the individual stories of my family and the forgotten human history of the Libyan people, as illustrated by Libyan folk poetry in the camps.[48] Since the 1930s, younger Libyans have orally passed the memory from one generation to the next. In light of these events, Libyans have developed a deep distrust of colonialism and Western policies in general. Critics of Italian neo-fascism focus on the fascist regime's (1922–45) anti-Semitic laws, but many commentators note that anti-Semitism developed late under the Italian fascists, and then only under pressure from Nazi Germany. It is this fact that produces the myth that Italian fascism was a more moderate rendition of fascism—a myth because it considers Italian fascism only in terms of Europe, ignoring the atrocities perpetuated in Libya and Ethiopia. The population of Libya was estimated at 1.5 million when the Italian conquest began in 1911. Of these, a half million died in battle or from disease, starvation, or thirst. Another 250,000 Libyans were forced into exile in Egypt, Chad, Tunisia, Turkey, Palestine, Syria, and Algeria. In 1935, the fascist colonial state drafted 20,000 young Libyans, including some young men who were interned with their parents in the concentration camps, to fight as a cheap labor force in the conquest of Ethiopia.

This is hardly a new policy; earlier, in 1911, the colonial state drafted over 20,000 Eritreans as soldiers to invade Libya.

We must never forget the evil deeds of the fascists both in Europe and in Libya. The notion of a *reformed fascism*—coinciding with the reemergence of Italy's neo-Fascist Party—is a dangerous new myth that no one should tolerate. A critical new study of Italian fascism must overcome the Eurocentric view of Italian fascism by looking at genocide in the colonies beyond Europe and insisting on the moral and political responsibility of the Italian state to open the archives so we can find how many skeletons are in the fascist closet.[49]

5

IDENTITY AND ALIENATION IN POSTCOLONIAL LIBYAN LITERATURE: THE TRILOGY OF AHMAD IBRAHIM AL-FAQIH

Western Imperialism and Third World nationalism feed each other but at their worst they are neither monolithic nor deterministic.

Edward W. Said, *Culture and Imperialism*

Allah will not oppress women and others, but men do that, especially simple men who are themselves victims of ignorance and injustice.

Sadiq al-Naihum, modernist Libyan essayist and critic,
Kalimat al-Haq al-Qawiyya

I sometimes find myself "examining my identity," as other people examine their conscience. As you may imagine, my object is not to discover within myself some "essential" allegiance in which I may recognize myself. Rather the opposite: I scour my memory to find as many ingredients of my identity as I can. I then assemble and arrange them. I don't deny any of them.

Amin Maalouf, *In the Name of Identity: Violence and the Need to Belong*

Literature, films, and oral traditions are important but often neglected resources for the study of social and political life in the Middle East. These unconventional resources provide a counterview to official state history.[1] Furthermore, writers in third world societies play a different role than their counterparts in Western societies. Like Latin American writers, Arab poets and novelists have been active in political and social challenges of postcolonial society and are taken very seriously by the public. One can note Taha Hussain, 'Abbas Mahmud al-'Akkad, Tawfiq al-Hakim, Naguib Mahfouz, Badr Shakir al-Sayyab, 'Abdulwahhab al-Bayati, Ahmad Fu'ad Najam, Mudhafar al-Nawab, and Nizar Qabani, to mention only a few influential Arab writers. These writers play a public role similar to the role played by American public intellectuals, such as Noam Chomsky, Cornel West, and Edward Said.

The need for cultural and social sources is even more urgent in the case of Libyan studies in the United States, where most of the journalistic and scholarly writings are characterized by a state-centered perspective, especially with respect to the persona of Colonel Muamar al-Qadhdhafi and terrorism. No state exists without a society, and unless one assumes that political leaders, like Qadhdhafi, are above society, then taking society seriously is an essential prerequisite for understanding any state.[2] Extending a study to include Libyan society and analyzing its diverse voices by exploring its literature will shed new light on where Qadhdhafi originates and how Libyan society has reacted to state policies. As a political scientist deeply involved with literature, one of my objectives is to recapture some neglected aspects of Libyan politics and culture. This essay attempts to introduce the magnum opus work of the leading Libyan writer Ahmad Ibrahim al-Faqih and to analyze how he interprets questions of identity, cultural encounter, and social alienation in contemporary Libya. But first, let me locate al-Faqih's work in the larger context of modern Libyan literature.

The short story was the dominant genre during the 1960s in Libya. Understanding the historical context of this genre may help readers appreciate the significance of Ahmad Ibrahim al-Faqih's trilogy. It is this genre that dominated creative writing—reflecting social change and capitalist urbanization—until novels began appearing in the

1970s. With themes of loss of community, alienation, and new class inequalities arising from oil discovery and migration to cities, short stories provide a literary and historical context for al-Faqih's work. Economic and cultural displacement—subjects favored by writers such as 'Abdallah al-Quwayri, Kamil al-Maqhur, Yusuf al-Sharif, Bashir al-Hashimi, and Ibrahim al-Kuni—are, in fact, universally understood as industry, technology, and ideologies have transformed nations. What is unique to Libya is that urbanization intensified in a society still dominated in the 1960s by strong kinship communities and weak large cities.

The focus of this chapter is the most recent work of al-Faqih, his trilogy *Sa Ahbiqa Madinatun Ukhra*, *Hadhihi Tukhum Mamlakati*, and *Nafaq Tudi'uhu 'Imra Wahida* (I shall present you with another city: I, These are the borders of my kingdom: II, and A tunnel lit by a woman: III, London: Riad al-Rayyes Books, 1991), which won the award for best novel in Beirut's book exhibition of 1992. Al-Faqih narrates the story of his childhood in the village of Mizda and in the city of Tripoli. The narrative reflects his perception of Libyan culture and politics under two regimes: the monarchy (1951–69) and the Republic/Jamahiriyya (after 1969). My focus is the novelist's responses to the social and cultural transformation and upheavals following the creation of the Libyan state, discovery of oil, and the military revolution of 1969. I argue that these changes put tremendous pressures on Libyan writers to find new forms to articulate their experiences and the new social realities they encountered. A review of Libyan literature since the 1960s is important to place al-Faqih's trilogy in the larger social and cultural context.

Al-Faqih (see Figure 5.1) is a middle-class modernist writer who belongs to what is called in Libya the "1960s generation." This group includes prominent Libyan fiction writers such al-Sadiq al-Naihum, Yusif al-Sharif, Ali al-Rgaii, Muhammad al-Shaltami, and Ibrahim al-Kuni. These writers began to publish poetry and short stories in the early 1960s.[3] Recently, al-Faqih and al-Kuni gained acclaim in the Arab world, and some of their works have been translated into other languages, such as Russian, German, Chinese, and English.[4] Al-Faqih received critical acclaim as one of the most talented short story writers in Libya. In 1965, his first collection of short stories, *Al-Bahr La ma'Fih* (There is no water in the sea), appeared in 1965 and won the highest award sponsored by the Royal Commission of Fine Arts in Libya.

Al-Faqih's work reflects themes of tension and conflict between rural village traditional, patriarchal life and individualistic, urban values. This was not surprising because Libyan society had just begun to

Figure 5.1 Ahmad Ibrahim al-Faqih, modern Libyan novelist, Cairo, Egypt, May 1998.

experience a deep process of urbanization and social change due to the impact of the new oil economy in the early 1960s.[5] Most Libyan writers of that period focused on the genre of the short story, and only when urban life became more complex in the late 1980s did the novel appear in Libyan literature. If the novel is the product of bourgeois capitalist society, then the emergence of the novel as a new genre in Libyan literature is a clear sign that a bourgeois middle class had developed in Libyan society.

The most prolific writer of his generation, al-Faqih has published eighteen books, ranging from plays and short stories to novels and nonfiction essays.[6] The trilogy is not only the culmination of his creative work and productive literary career but displays many similarities to the author's life. In fact, the name of the main protagonist, Khalil al-Imam, resembles the author's name. Khalil is the nickname for Ibrahim, and Imam is a synonym for Faqih in Arabic. Furthermore, Khalil al-Imam, the hero of the trilogy, like the novelist, was born in a Libyan village, moved to Tripoli, and studied theater and literature in Great Britain.

Understanding that most readers are not aware of his work, brief biographical notes of al-Faqih are appropriate before analyzing the themes presented in his trilogy. Al-Faqih was born on December 28, 1932, in a small village in western Tripolitania, called Mizda, which is located 100 miles south of the city of Tripoli. He studied in his village until the age of fifteen when he moved to Tripoli, the capital and largest city in the country. In 1962 he left Libya for Egypt to study journalism in a UNESCO program and then returned to Tripoli to work as a journalist. Between 1962 and 1971, he was offered a scholarship to study theater in London. When he came back to Libya in 1972, he was appointed head of the National Institute of Music and Drama. In 1972, al-Faqih became the editor of the influential *Cultural Weekly.* After that, he returned to England as a Libyan diplomat and began to study for his doctorate in literature. In 1990, he finished his degree and returned to North Africa, where he now divides his time between residences in Cairo and Rabat.[7]

This trilogy, al-Faqih's most ambitious and mature work, presents Khalil al-Imam, a Libyan student who goes to the University of Edinburgh in Scotland to study for his doctorate in literature. His dissertation topic is the impact of Arabic myths on English literature, specifically sex and violence in the folk tales of *The Arabian Nights.* The first book of the trilogy takes place in Scotland, where Khalil is thrown into a world of foreigners, especially women, and tries to find a way to deal with the new culture. In the second volume, Khalil goes back to his country, Libya, to teach at Tripoli University. There, as in England, he runs into emotional problems and becomes severely depressed. With the help of a Muslim healer, he experiences an exciting Sufi spiritual journey to a utopian city of the past. But because of his unpredictable pride and self confidence, he destroys his happiness by opening the forbidden door and hence finds himself back in the city of concrete reality, Tripoli, where he faces the reality of Libyan society while vainly attempting to find his own identity. This trilogy dramatizes, through fantasy, the depth of the social and political alienation of some Western-educated Libyan intellectuals in the postcolonial period.[8] The problem of Western-inspired alienation in Libyan society is shared by many Arab and third world intellectuals, but this is a special case because in Libyan society it has not been explored in a setting that is still opposed to the modern nation-state.

Al-Faqih begins the three books of his trilogy with the statement, "A time has passed and another time is not coming," and ends the third book with an equally pessimistic statement, "A time has passed and another time has not come and will never come." He is doubtful about the possibility of positive change, because as long as the existing social and political conditions are perpetuated, society, like Khalil, is stalled. The trilogy deals effectively with the social and political causes of such pessimism and the problems experienced by Khalil, who is torn between the values of a traditional, patriarchal life in the village and a contemporary individualistic life in the city. At the very beginning, Khalil enters a new city, Edinburgh. As he is looking for a room to rent, he comes across a couple, Linda and Donald, in whose home he rents a room.

One night Linda comes to his room and they begin a love affair. Donald, who is interested in Eastern philosophies, does not mind sharing Linda with Khalil. To further complicate his personal life, Khalil meets another woman at the university, Sandra, who plays Desdemona to Khalil's Othello in the student theater. One night after rehearsal he and Sandra get drunk and, the next morning, he finds her next to him in his bed. When Linda discovers the affair, she decides to end her relationship with Khalil. But Linda becomes pregnant and Khalil realizes that because Donald is impotent, he is the true father of the child. Khalil tries to go back to Linda, but she refuses. He becomes torn between the two women. Linda decides to leave Donald and go back to her parents with Khalil's child, Adam. In the meantime, Sandra is kidnapped by members of a youth gang, who brutally rape her and leave her near death. Fortunately, she is saved and taken to the hospital. Only then does Khalil discover that Sandra's father is a millionaire. Khalil finishes his doctorate on sex and violence in *The Arabian Nights*, which echoes the same disturbed emotions of his real-life encounters with Linda and Sandra. He remembers his family and country and decides to go back to Libya, leaving behind his child, Adam, with Linda. The symbolic meaning of this section in the novel is the creation of a bond between Libyan and British cultures. The name of the child (Adam) signifies the common origins of mankind—Adam and Eve. Khalil's attempt to pursue love and adopt the values of Western society fail, however, due to his unpredictable cravings and his inability to choose between Linda and Sandra. In the end he loses both women. The book takes place in the early 1970s, a turning point in Libyan history when the revolutionary military regime not only toppled the pro-British monarchy, but also closed British and American military bases in Libya.

The second book of the trilogy begins, again, with the statement, "A time has passed and another time is not coming." By repeating the same statement, the novelist reminds the reader that Khalil is still trapped in a continuous state of hopelessness. Khalil returns to Tripoli where he becomes a professor at Tripoli University. Because of family pressure, he agrees to marry Fatima, a schoolteacher, to prove his membership in a society that expects young men and women to be married at an early age. However, after three years in this loveless marriage, he becomes very depressed.[9] He tries modern therapy, but doctors are unable to figure out the cause of his severe psychological illness. Out of desperation, he accepts his brother's advice to see a Muslim healer, a Sufi *faqih*, for treatment.

Desperate for a cure, Khalil goes to his childhood neighborhood in the old city of Tripoli to meet Faqih Sadiq Abu al-Khayrat, whose name, literally translated in English, means "truthful the father of good life." Notice the significance of this name for Khalil. Modern medicine cannot cure Khalil's depression because his illness is not physiological but emotional and spiritual.[10] Only a Muslim healer, whose name and specialties are truth and the meaning of good life, can help him. Faqih Abu al-Khayrat burns some frankincense and recites verses from the Quran. Suddenly, Khalil finds himself in an eleventh-century B.C. utopian city called "Necklace of Jewels," reminiscent of a city in *The Arabian Nights*. This fantastic city has no prisons, no taxes, no police, and no wages. Life is communal and production is shared. This is a subtle critique of the Arab state, which relies on secret police and the repression of intellectuals and freedom of expression.[11] According to tradition, he marries the princess, Narjiss of the Hearts, and becomes the prince of the city. The princess warns him not to enter a secret room in the palace, as the ancestors have warned people about the curse of the room.

Khalil finds happiness and love in the city of dreams. Then, disturbingly, he meets Budur, a beautiful singer. He falls in love with her, and as in the case of the first book, is torn between two women, Narjiss and Budur. Also, as in the case of Linda (in the first book), Khalil discovers that Narjiss is pregnant with his child. One must remember that Linda and Narjiss both conceived children with Khalil, while his Libyan wife, Fatima, cannot bear children. Love seems to be associated with fertility in the novel, and since Khalil does not love his wife, she cannot bear children with him but worst for him is that his reckless desire leads him to open the door of the secret room. A nasty yellow wind blasts from the room and he suddenly finds himself back again in the present in the city of Tripoli. He realizes he has been in a dream—a beautiful one that he has destroyed. Khalil is unable to commit himself to a normal loving relationship even when he lives in a dreamlike utopian city. Therefore, he returns to brutal reality and back to his life in Tripoli.

The third volume of the trilogy takes place in the city of reality, Tripoli. His wife, Fatima, wants a child, but he is not interested. Once again he becomes depressed and alienated from his wife's family and from his boring job at the university. Before slipping into a deeper depression, however, he meets Sana Amir, a beautiful and intelligent pharmacy graduate student at the University of Tripoli. She becomes the woman who lights up his life as the title of the third book of the trilogy indicates (*Nafaq Tudi'uhu*, A tunnel lit by a woman). When Fatima discovers her husband's new love, Khalil insists on a divorce; Fatima demands ownership of the flat, which Khalil does not mind relinquishing.

Khalil becomes a free and happy man in love with Sana. One day he meets his childhood friend, Jum'a Abu Khatwa, who attends al-Azhar University but returned to Tripoli to become a singer with the stage name Anwar Jalal. Anwar invites Khalil to his night parties where he discovers the fun life of music, dance, sex, and drinking. Despite the fact that alcohol, drugs, and premarital sex are restricted by state laws, Anwar's parties are frequented and protected by state officials, who seem to be alienated from the official claims of Islamic purity.[12] Khalil sarcastically chastises the hypocrisy of a society where "people in his city burn trees and replace them with pillars of cement, and where camels are slaughtered and replaced by big iron insects called cars."[13] Through Khalil's character, the novelist expresses his distaste not only for some of the tribal and Islamic laws but also the new consumerism of the modern oil economy, because it marginalizes individuals like Khalil who do not fit in (i.e., intellectuals like Khalil became consumers of services and imported goods). Khalil is now completely alienated from what he views as the rigid social values of honor and family. He finds the university restrictive and plagued by corruption. One day he drives his car around the city of Tripoli thinking, "My city is no longer a village but not yet a city, not Eastern or Western; it does not belong to the past nor to the present, between the desert and the sea, between past time and a time that is not coming."[14] This is a significant statement as it expresses the middle-class, cosmopolitan, and modernist views of al-Faqih toward his city; it also shows that Libyan society is dominated by hinterland rural forces. He struggles with his society's history and the hegemony of the rural and tribal forces of the hinterland over the weak urban centers. Libya is different from other eastern Arab societies such as Egypt, Syria, Palestine, and Lebanon, where notables and large landowners in big urban cities (e.g., Cairo, Damascus, and Beirut) dominate the countryside. Libya has had two leaders since independence, King Idriss al-Sanusi and Muamar al-Qadhdhafi, both of whom came from and were supported by hinterland social forces.[15] This historical context is essential to understanding the causes of alienation for a Western-educated intellectual such as Khalil al-Imam, who finds his escape in alcohol, sex, and music. The problem of intellectual displacement from their own societies is not unique to al-Faqih and is shared by many people from third world countries. The causes of this displacement are culture and social class. Third world societies experienced capitalist colonization by European states and found themselves struggling to determine their identity whereas many third world intellectuals have come from a middle- or upper-class background, and therefore look down on their own peasant/tribal cultures by using the language of modernity and progress.

Plagued by his conflicting desires in his real city, Khalil cannot wait to be happy with Sana, the woman who now lights his passage through life, but in a wild destructive moment he tries to rape her in his apartment. She leaves him and he must now face himself and his problems. Torn between dreams and reality, he can no longer teach and the university fires him. He becomes a regular member of Anwar's group, and the trilogy ends with the statement, "A time has passed, another is not coming and will never come." Although the ending is sad and pessimistic, it is nonetheless realistic. Khalil's life and his society are still full of contradictions, and there can be no change in Khalil's life as long as these contradictions exist.

Many other Arab writers have dealt with these questions before, from the Egyptian Tawfiq al-Haqim to the Sudanese al-Tayib Salih.[16] Like the Sudan, Libya was Italy's colony from 1911 to 1943; and from 1943 to 1951 it was occupied by the British and French armies, who defeated the German and Italian forces in the destructive battles of World War II. Libyan independence was the product of rivalry between the allies. At the beginning of the Cold War, the strategic location of Libya was crucial for the British and American interests, especially after the 1948 war in Palestine, the Nasser's revolution in Egypt in 1952, and the nationalization of the Suez Canal in 1956. Two other factors were also important: the demands of the exiled Libyan leaders in Egypt for independence and the support of their demands by the Arab League. These interests were not the same.

The British policy was hostile to the Tripolitanian nationalists' demands for a unified country and their close ties with the Arab League. Only when a diplomatic alliance between the gradualist and pragmatist Amir Idriss al-Sanusi, the exiled leader of the defeated Sanusiyya order, and the British colonial in Egypt was established, did Libyan independence became a real possibility. In 1951, England and the United States engineered the creation of an independent Libyan state in exchange for a political alliance with military bases on Libyan soil. Political parties were banned and the leader of the Tripolitanian Congress Party, Bashir al-Sadawi, was stripped of his citizenship and sent into exile in 1953.

Libyan independence was a major turning point for the Libyan people, but such independence brought many contradictions. The monarchy faced the heavy task of building a nationhood and interacting with the international system after a brutal colonization under the Italians, which led to the death of half of the population including the educated elite. A Libyan state was created but without strong Libyan nationhood. The monarchy was dominated by tribal *shaykhs* and urban notables. The state was one of the poorest in the world with a per capita gross national product (GNP) of $35 and a 90 percent illiteracy rate (one of the highest illiteracy rates in the world in 1951). The state was dependent on economic aid and rent from British and American military bases. The political structure of Libya was designed by the United Nations as a federal constitutional monarchy with three regional states. The aloof King Idriss lived in Tubruq next to a British military base in eastern Libya, and favored his eastern region, Barqa, even though the population of this region constituted only 27 percent of the total population of the country (Tripolitania's population represented 68 percent and Fezzan, the southern region, 5 percent).

The discovery and the exportation of oil in 1961 had a major economic and social impact on the country. Suddenly the Libyan state, which was one of the poorest, became one of the richest in Africa and the Middle East. The monarchy initiated various programs in education, health, transportation, and housing. A new Libyan university was opened in 1955 with two campuses in Benghazi and Tripoli. By the late 1960s, the educational policies led to the rise of a new salaried middle class, a militant student movement, a small working class, trade unions, and modern intellectuals such as al-Faqih. The Sanusi monarchy lasted from 1951 until 1969, when a military coup replaced it and declared it a republic, and in 1977, the name of Libya was changed to Jamahiriyya ("the state of the masses" in English).

During the old regime, Libya shared close educational, economic, and military ties with the West, especially England and the United States. Libyan students were sent to these countries and Egypt rather than to Russia or China. Therefore, Khalil al-Imam's trip to Scotland is the result of the colonial and cultural hegemony of Great Britain over Libya after 1943. Al-Faqih's trilogy is similar to al-Tayib Salih's novel, *Season of the Migration to the North* (Portsmouth, NH: Heinemann, 1970). Both examine the dislocation and alienation of Arab men and their confrontation with westernization and modernity yet they do so using different overtones: Sudanese and Libyan. Salih's novel deals with the impact of colonial dislocation, while al-Faqih's trilogy, two decades later, is concerned with postcolonial nationalist culture.

The roots of a torn personality such as Khalil's are not found in the traveling genre of the Arabic novel that focus mainly on East/West encounters but in the protagonist's fundamental alienation from his own society. Khalil is moody, unpredictable, and violent, like the topic of his doctoral dissertation. That is why the novel is as complex and multifaceted as Tayib Salih's *Season of the Migration to the North*. Like Mustafa Said, a brilliant Sudanese Muslim student who lived in England and was haunted by sex and violence due to Sudan's colonial experience, Khalil al-Imam also faces violence and uncertainties in Great Britain and at home in northern Sudan and western Libya. Moreover, the Libyan novelist brilliantly adopts the style and narration of *The Arabian Nights*, especially in the first and second books. It must be remembered that unlike poetry, the novel was a new literary form in Libya, but like other Arab novelists, al-Faqih used Arab and Libyan voices during a time of capitalist transformation.

But what are the roots of Khalil's troubles and unpredictability, especially his feelings toward women? The novelist suggests that Khalil's problem is one of culture and class. Al-Faqih gives the reader a clue from Khalil's childhood in the village. Khalil almost dies because the man who circumcises him uses an unclean knife, which causes an inflammation of the penis. Due to the lack of medical care and rampant poverty in the village, Khalil cannot be treated before migrating with his family to the city of Tripoli. The physical problem of his penis is a metaphor for the wounded patriarchal male identity to which Khalil refers in the trilogy: "This penis which I almost lost due to my circumcision is the only thing that Sana does not have."[17] Khalil uses violence and sex with women to assert his personality and male ego. He elaborates more by stating, "I know that sex is natural, but I pursue it with a psychology that carries with it old wounds of tribal societies that migrated to the cities. I love and hate every woman. I hold them responsible for the feeling of shame I felt after each time I masturbated. These feelings are the ones that destroyed my relationship with Linda and Sana."[18] This is the root of his sexual and social troubles. He becomes aware of it when he travels to Britain, and therefore, is distanced from Libyan culture and is able to reflect on his native society. Khalil's disillusionment is also political because he is alienated from his society, his tribe, his family, the university, and the state. He blames all of them for his emotional, sexual, and political alienation.

The trilogy explodes with all of these contradictions and gives no direct clue as to how they can be resolved. According to the author, there can be no happy ending to this complex novel, not until Libyan society itself resolves these conflicts. The author does not apologize for these contradictions, nor does he create a happy ending for his novel. Indeed, these are not unique contradictions; other societies experiencing colonialism, economic transformation, and social and cultural dislocation suffer the same challenges. What seems unique to Libyan society is its persistent autonomous kinship and Islamic social organizations, its weak urban centers, and its reluctance to adopt the modern nation-state. Ibrahim al-Faqih dramatizes these cultural and social conflicts from a middle-class modernist perspective and consequently brings Libyan society into contemporary history.

The novel suggests that the complexity facing Libyan society and culture is a reflection of transition from tributary, rural values to urban capitalist society. While al-Faqih focuses on the contradictions of urbanization and the pain of adopting a new identity in Libya and European cities, Ibrahin al-Kuni, the other well-known Libyan novelist, focuses instead on the rural and nomadic people of the Libyan Sahara. Despite the fact that the modern novel was born in and is often about modern cities, al-Kuni's novels are about modern people but not city people. These two novelists explore Libyan culture and identities from different perspectives. Al-Faqih gives us the views of urban cities in Libya while al-Kuni opens another window to the rural and desert culture of Libya.

6

THE JAMAHIRIYYA: HISTORICAL AND SOCIAL
ORIGINS OF A POPULIST STATE

This hegemony of the idea of the modern nation-state has created
a clear political paradox in the debates on the state today. The
new critics find the concept of the modern state looking more
and more tired, out of line with realities, and unable to cope with
the new problems and threats to human survival. Yet, in the
meanwhile, the concept has acquired immense institutional
power and a wide base in the global mass culture.

> Ashis Nandy, "State," in Wolfgang Sachs, ed., *The
> Development Dictionary: A Guide to Knowledge as Power*

The turning point for the historian of modern Libya is the whole
dependence of the Libyan people (after the discovery of oil in
1960) individuals and groups, males and females, on a small
organ called the state.

> Sadiq al-Naihum, modernist Libyan essayist and critic,
> *Kalimat al-Haq al-Qawiyya*

You cannot take down a mountain with a hammer.

> Libyan proverb

INTRODUCTION

With the exception of a few recent studies of the Libyan state, little is known in the United States about the internal social and political structure, and particularly the interaction between state and society in Libya. After independence in 1951, and up until the military revolution in 1969, the Libyan state was described in the same terms used by Eurocentric scholars to depict other North African states: modernizing, patrimonial, and segmentary. Marxist scholarship viewed precolonial North Africa, including Libya, as an Asiatic source of production. When a group of junior officers led by Muammar Qadhdhafi toppled the Sanusi monarchy on September 1, 1969 and the oil crisis of 1973 led eventually to confrontation between the Reagan administration and the revolutionary regime in Tripoli, Libya gained visibility in the international news. However, most journalistic and scholarly writings on Libya have fixated on the persona of Colonel Muammar al-Qadhdhafi, characterizing him as "a mad Dog" heading a "terrorist rogue and pariah state." (The usual definition of *rogue* encompasses three elements commonly mentioned in writing about the Libyan leader: viciousness, lack of principle, and propensity to engage in unilateral action.) The American obsession with Qadhdhafi reduces the entire Libyan state and its politics to Qadhdhafi, with the result that Qadhdhafi and the Libyan Jamahiriyya government are often seen as an aberration rather than a product of recognizable social forces. Libyan social history, society, and culture tend to be mentioned only in passing or completely ignored.[1]

This myopic analysis cannot explain why the Qadhdhafi government, despite American sanctions and diplomatic isolation, has not collapsed as did the Sanusi monarchy and other African states. Demonization of Qadhdhafi and his government has, in fact, been one of the major barriers to scholarly analysis of this enigmatic African state.[2]

This final chapter has three main goals in challenging mainstream images, while providing an alternative personal and theoretical conceptualization of the Libyan state and society. First, it presents a review and evaluation of the existing political literature on the modern Libyan state. Second, it offers a historical narrative on the origins and transformation of Libya based on the internal dynamics of its society. Third, it provides conclusions based on the Libyan experience.

THEORETICAL APPROACHES TO COLONIAL AND POSTCOLONIAL STATES

A brief analysis of the scholarship on North Africa or the Maghrib is essential to understanding Libyan politics. Maghribi studies have been dominated by scholars concerned with French and Italian colonial studies, British social anthropology, and American modernization theories. With French and Italian studies focusing mainly on the need within the colonial states to manage the natives, it comes as no surprise that many researchers were colonial officers. In their view, precolonial society was simply traditional, with rural areas inhabited by unruly tribesmen and towns governed by corrupt patrimonial states. According to this analytic framework, tribesmen and townsmen rarely cooperated.[3]

The most influential approach to Maghribi studies has been the segmentary model articulated by British social anthropologists E. E. Evans-Pritchard and Ernest Gellner. This model assumes the existence of a tribal society comprised of homogenous tribal segments. In the absence of state control, order was maintained through mutually deterring internal segments within any clan threatening to disrupt the balance of power. The segmentary model, like colonial literature, perceives precolonial Maghrib society as an agglomeration of tribes or tribal states basically isolated from the larger social and economic structures of the region.[4]

Scholars of the segmentary model view the social history of Libya as a variation on the theme of statelessness—the absence of a central state in both the early and modern periods. They base this theory on the persistence of regional and tribal federations that prevailed until the second half of the twentieth century. The fact that these so-called changeless tribal forces produced a strong society with a dynamic social history is largely ignored. In other words, if one does not assume the necessity for a centralized state, its absence does not necessarily constitute a sign of weakness, but is rather an indicator of different regional social formations providing structural institutions that represent a type of state formation.[5]

Modernization theorists like Daniel Lerner consider the present-day Maghrib to be composed of traditional societies that began to modernize under European colonialism. This interpretation holds that traditional tribal and religious values can be expected to fade and be replaced by modern, Western, "rational" values. Despite colonization and modernization under the postcolonial states, however, Mahgribi societies are suffering from economic inefficiencies, family and military rule, and instead of secularization, a resurgence of political Islam in Algeria, Tunisia, Libya and, to a lesser degree, Morocco.[6]

Eurocentric Marxist scholars, such as Eve Lacoste, view the precolonial Maghrib as a case of the classical "Asiatic mode of production." Briefly, this notion assumes the existence of a strong state and self-sufficient village communities. Marx's views of the area relied on a sketchy orientalist image of India. In addition, his assumption of change came mainly from the outside, in the form of European capitalist colonialization, and appears uninfluenced by his normal dialectical approach. In general, the concept of the Asiatic mode of production is inadequate because it is based on a vague knowledge of India, Asia, and Africa, and denies the preexistence of private property, describes a strong state without the existence of social classes, and finally, omits dialectical analysis. The precolonial Maghribi states clearly do not fit this Asiatic model.[7]

In summary, the literature on North Africa suffers from two major deficiencies. First, the Eurocentric view of Maghribi society assumes all change flows from Europe or the West—the "rational," revolutionary, and detribalized region that produced modern capitalist transformation. This line of reasoning ignores diverse traditions of state formation in Africa and negates the voices of a fluid social history in Africa prior to the colonial period. Fundamentally simplistic, it reduces North African social history to some changeless tribal structure-creating force that somehow emanates from the Muslim mind.

The second inadequacy of the literature, especially modernization theory, is its inability to explain social transformation and the nature of politics in today's North Africa. Despite capitalist colonialization and postcolonial modernization, one is struck by the persistence of noncapitalist modes of production, such as sharecropping, tribal communal ownership of land, and self-sufficiency in household production, which continued as late as the 1970s and was especially true in Libya and Morocco. Further, instead of the secularization predicted by modernization scholars, social and political Islamic movements emerged as the main oppositional forces in Egypt, Algeria, and Tunisia and are now gaining support in Libya and Morocco.[8] An alternative analysis would explain the durability of the current Libyan state as a result of its ability to mobilize human resources through transformation of the economy and society.

The role of the African state is exaggerated when taken as the starting point of political and social analysis instead of looking at the state from within (i.e., from the point of view of African societies). In his analysis of the social process of the colonial state, Bjorn Beckman articulated this perspective: the analysis of state/civil society relations must start from what has historically constituted the state at the level of civil society. What are society's demands of the state, and how has the state developed in response to such demands? The fact that the postcolonial state was inherited from colonialism does not make it any more detached from society than any other state. While originally having developed in response to the requirements of colonial interests, transformations at the level of local society internalized these demands of society. The contradictions generated by transformations created new sets of demands on the state, which it sought to manage, combining promotion, repression, and other means of regulation. Colonial and other foreign capital had primary stakes in the state, and they continue to do so. The state offers protection and services. While neoliberal more than radical theorizing can be blamed for obscuring this relation, the latter tends to neglect the manner in which seemingly external determinants of the state were internalized into local civil society. While Cadbury, the chocolate manufacturers, wanted the colonial state to protect its interests, the cocoa farmers organized in their own defense, pressuring the state. The colonial state, which was very rudimentary at inception, was itself formed as part of this process. Some of the interests in the state had precolonial origins, seeking protection, for instance, for preexisting relations of power and privilege. Others represented emerging social forces that challenged the traditional relations of production and their mutations under colonialism, as well as new ones, specific to the colonial economy and society. In its management of these contradictions, the colonial state developed its own "popular roots."[9]

RECLAIMING LIBYAN SOCIAL HISTORY

Recasting the Libyan state requires placing Libyan society as the starting point. From this perspective, a number of questions should be raised. How has Libyan society viewed the colonial and postcolonial state? Can society manage without a state? What are the historical and social processes that produced the Jamahiriyya state? Is it the only option? And why did this political experiment in creating an indigenous state stall by the mid-1980s?

Three points should be kept in mind here. First, the 1969 revolution led by Qadhdhafi was not an anomaly as many Western journalists and scholars think, but firmly rooted in the hinterland society of the Sanusiyya and the Tripolitanian Republic with their pan-Islamic culture, kinship autonomous organizations, fear of the central state, and mistrust of the West based on bitter colonial experience under Italy. Qadhdhafi was able to articulate and transform anticolonial resistance and Libyan nationalism by translating these legacies into a revolutionary ideology using down-to-earth language understood by ordinary Libyans. Qadhdhafi used his charisma brilliantly to mobilize people and attack his opponents and rivals inside and outside Libya. He speaks and dresses like a tribesman—a *badawi*—from the hinterland, and leads prayers as an Imam or Amir al Muminin ("the prince of the faithful"). By appealing to the rural ideology of statelessness and fear of the urban-centered state (seen as the colonial state), Qadhdhafi destroyed institutions of the old monarchy and, at the same time, created the Jamahiriyya institutions legitimizing a strong state acceptable to most Libyans in the hinterland. He often mocks the old regime and the Western institutions that were imposed on Libya by the United Nations and the Great Powers (United Kingdom, France, and the United States) in 1951.

To weaken urban opposition among students, intellectuals, and the old bourgeoisie in the big cities, the new regime even pursued a cultural policy of *Bedwanization*, attacking urban values and encouraging rural rituals based on tribal values concerning dress, music, and festivals. As a result of a systematic de-urbanization policy, the city of Tripoli—the most urban and cosmopolitan in the country—lost its former character. Yet the Jamahiriyya is a populist modern state. It is by no means a return to the pristine past. By populism, I refer to the movement of the propertied middle class, which mobilizes the lower classes with radical rhetoric against imperialism, foreign capitalism, and the political establishment.[10] The political experiment of the Jamahiriyya ("state of the masses") in Libya, therefore, would make sense if one looked carefully at the historical and cultural bases of Libyan society.

The second point is that the Jamahiriyya government received wide public support among the lower and middle classes, which allowed the government to engage in a major transformation of the economy as well as the social and political structure. Third, and equally important, internal and external opposition to the government led to more repressive actions against its opponents by the early 1980s. These repressive actions gave more power to the security apparatus of the state and marginalized newly created public institutions, such as popular committees and people's congresses. With the Jamahiriyya becoming like other states in the region—a national security state—the social base of the regime narrowed and a militant, armed Islamic opposition began challenging the government in the early 1990s. Now the regime seems to have exhausted its revolutionary zeal and faces major domestic problems, including a lack of institutionalization, weakened civil associations, brain drain of the best-educated Libyans, and an inability on the part of its leadership to deal with a changing, complex international system.

Discussion of the origins of Libya evokes personal experiences that influence my work as a Libyan-born political scientist. My childhood in the social and cultural environment of central and southern Libya was shaped by family memories of upheavals, wars, defeats, and resistance during the colonial period between 1911 and 1943. The generation that lived through that period, as my grandparents did, or the generation that witnessed its last phase and the birth of the Libyan state in 1951, as my parents did, passed on to their children a vivid oral history of their displacements, anguish, and struggle for survival. The hinterland culture of my family emphasizes a deep mistrust of the West as a result of the harsh colonial experience, loss of Islamic and Arab identity, and autonomy from the state. I overcame this one-dimensional view when I came to the United States to study in 1980.

My generation lived through the independent Libyan state of the monarchy of King Idriss al-Sanusi and the Qadhdhafi revolution of 1969. Without the Qadhdhafi government's populist policies, I would not have been able to study in Egypt and the United States. As a result of the revolutionary government's encouragement and equal opportunities for high school students from the hinterland to compete for university scholarships, I was trained as a political scientist at the Faculty of Economics and Political Science of Cairo University in Egypt and the University of Washington in Seattle in the United States. Inevitably, as I chose to write about state formation and Libyan social history in the twentieth century, I found myself relying more and more on certain elements of this lived history.

As a graduate student in the United States, my first attempt to examine theories of state–society relations used Weberian and structural-functionalist theories in which kinship and ideology are assumed to be separate from social and economic conditions. This methodology did not provide convincing answers to the question of why noncapitalist relations of production (agrarian, traditional economic and social relations such as bartering, sharecropping, and communal ownerership of land) persisted in Libya after the colonial period.[11] Several apparent historical discrepancies among the three regions of Libya (Tripolitania, Barqa, and Fezzan) also became increasingly puzzling to me. Why, for example, did the coastal towns—with the exception of Tripoli—play an economic and political role subordinate to that of the hinterland tribes and peasants? Why and how were the hinterland tribes and peasants able to resist both the Ottoman and Italian colonial states up through the 1930s? Why did Barqa (the eastern region) have no major urban centers in the precolonial period?

Inspired by the works of Ibn Khaldun, Antonio Gramsci, E. P. Thompson, and James Scott, I adopted a political and moral economy approach. This approach has the advantage of linking economics to politics by analyzing the relationships among ecology, production, and the land tenure system, as well as the legal, cultural, and social structures. Class is defined as a social and cultural formation, and culture should be approached as a process rather than a static or essential concept.

In my book on state formation and social history in Libya between 1830 and 1932, I reached some conclusions essential for understanding the postcolonial state after 1951.[12]

- First, the local response to the Ottoman and Italian states was both determined and circumscribed by the imperatives of social organization in Libya's three regions.
- Second, powerful tribal and peasant alliances ruled Libya before the Ottomans, when construction of a modern urban centralized state began. Because local institutions built by the Sanusiyya movement and the Ottoman Empire were destroyed by the Italian state, Libyan society had strong regional identities and associated the urban central state with the hated Italian colonial state.
- Third, displacement of the Ottoman Empire by Italian colonialism in 1912 renewed the need for tribal-peasant confederations as governing centers, and explains their dominance over social life after independence in 1951.
- Fourth, the process of incorporating Libya into the colonial capitalist world system was not a linear progression from precapitalist to capitalist relations. The process was, in fact, resisted and modified during the colonial period. Sufi Islam, tribal-peasant military organizations, and oral traditions were all crucial social and cultural weapons in the fight against Italian colonialism.[13]

THE RISE OF REGIONAL STATES

There are a number of reasons why focusing on the central state is not helpful in understanding the origins of Libya and would not reveal the country's unequal and diverse social development. Barqa had a separate regional political economy from the tribes of the hinterland, which had weak political and economic ties with towns from 1830 to 1870. Their natural market for agropastoral surplus was western Egypt. After 1870, the rise of the Sanusi order as a major power in Barqa deepened the autonomy of the hinterland, an indigenous state based on a pan-Islamic model, taxes, laws, and tribal customs. The Sanusiyya built a decentralized structural order based on trade and Sufi institutions, which eventually became a skeleton state. In 1911, urban notables tied to foreign capital brought Tripolitanian peasants and tribesmen into European markets through Italian and British investments. At the same time, the relative hegemony of the Ottoman state over the countryside explains cooperation between some of the urban notables and rural tribesmen and peasants against the Italians. When the Ottoman Empire signed a peace treaty with Italy and withdrew its forces from Libya, the Sanusi leadership declared itself a state, and in 1920, the Italian colonial state recognized the Sanusi Emirate in Barqa.

By 1911, Tripolitania in the western region of Libya was in transition from a trading and tributary political economy to capitalism in response to Ottoman state formation, decline of the Sahara trade, and penetration of British and Italian capital. Tripolitanian notables fought over bureaucratic positions in the Ottoman state as well as land and revenues from foreign firms. By 1915, unified forces of the three regions of Libya defeated the Italian army, and in 1918, the first republic in the region was declared. Factionalism continued between 1918 and 1924, however, among Tripolitanian notables as a result of capitalist penetration.

The Tripolitanian Republic was the second indigenous state to emerge in Libya after the Sanusi Emirate in the Eastern region. The republic was rooted in a pan-Islamic ideology and led collectively by four notables since the Tripolitanian notables and tribal *shaykhs* could not agree on one leader. The republic's four founding fathers included Ramadan al-Suwayhli (eastern Tripolitania), Sulayman al-Baruni (a former Ottoman senator from Jabal al-Gharbi in the west), Ahmad al-Murayyid (central area), and 'Abd al-Nabi Bilkhayr (eastern hinterland). 'Abd al-Rahman Azzam, the Egyptian pan-Arab nationalist and subsequently the first secretary general of the Arab League, served as an advisor to the republic.

The new government was very popular throughout Tripolitania but received little support from the Great Powers. Messages to France, England, and Italy requesting diplomatic recognition based on self-determination resulted in limited autonomy accorded by Italy but no response from the other Great Powers, despite an appeal that was eventually recognized under President Woodrow Wilson's famous Declaration of the Right of Nations for Self Determination in 1919. At the same period and like other anticolonial movements in Africa, the republic achieved some important gains from the colonial state: internal autonomy, guarantees of civil liberties, central representation in local governments, and indigenous control of most of the local administration in the hinterland. These gains did not last long as the fascist movement took power in Rome and formed a new regime.

In 1922, the new fascist government in Rome declared war and abrogated its agreements with the two antagonist states—the Sanusi Emirate and the Tripolitanian Republic. The Tripolitanian Republic was defeated in 1924, but the Sanusi forces continued a guerrilla war until 1932. Facing defeat and lacking political allies, the Republic's leaders voted in 1922 to declare a *Bay'a*, which meant giving consent to Amir Idriss al-Mahdi al Sanusi, the head of the Sanusiyya, to serve as Amir for a unified Libyan government. The proposal created a dilemma for Amir Idriss. If he accepted the Tripolitanian offer, he would anger the Italians who had recognized the Sanusi Emirate in 1920. Shrewdly, his decision was to accept the *Bay'a* but leave Barqa for exile in Egypt. By 1932, the fascist armies controlled the whole country. Most of the leaders of the resistance were either killed or exiled to Tunisia, Egypt, Chad, Palestine, Syria, and Turkey.

The Libyan colonial experience leaves us with two important issues: the persistence of regionalism and the legacy of two indigenous state formations, the Sanusi Emirate and the Tripolitanian Republic.

NATIONALISM AND LIBYAN INDEPENDENCE

Contrary to the essentially nationalist Libyan historiography of recent years, use of the terms *Libya* and *Libyans* when referring to the nineteenth century should be understood as referring to the Ottoman regency of Tarabulus al-Gharb, and not suggest the contemporary nation-state that emerged in 1951. This tendency is common to many nationalist movements. As Mahmood Mamdani stated, "Hence the insistence on distinguishing the popular nationalism of the 1940s from the statist nationalism of the 1960s and 1970s, and on underlining the fact that whereas the former went hand in hand with democratic struggle, the latter was not only divorced from it but was even turned into the spearhead for legitimizing and demobilizing social movements with democratic potential."[14]

The Libyan modern nation-state is a recent construction and a product of the colonial period and reaction to its impact. The very name *Libya* was revived by Italian colonialists in 1911 from nomenclature in Greek and Roman times. This revival was in fact an integral part of the policy justifying colonialism by linking it with the Roman rule of the Mediterranean.

Italian colonialism ended in 1943 when the Allies defeated the German and Italian armies in Libya. Libyan independence was born of rivalry between the Allies. At the beginning of the Cold War, the strategic location of Libya was crucial to British and American interests, especially after the Gamal 'Abdul Nasser revolution in Egypt in 1952. Two other factors played an important role: the demand of the exiled

Libyan leaders in Egypt for Libyan independence, and the Arab League's support of that demand. These interests were not the same. Only when a diplomatic alliance between the gradualist and pragmatic Amir Idriss al-Sanusi, the exiled third leader of the defeated Sanusiyya order, and the British colonial powers in Egypt was established, did Libyan independence become a real possibility. Such independence was engineered and dominated by the British. Historian Jacques Roumani captures the drama and the politics of the birth of the Libyan state when he states succinctly, "The new independent Libya was thus the product of a reluctant partnership between two distinct political legacies, the republic which carried the tradition of the 1915 revolt and the Sanusi Emirate which departed from it. Both can be credited with important achievements: the Emirate for introducing Libya to the mechanics of statehood and the gains of diplomacy; the republic for making the earliest bid for indigence independence and pursuing it despite international quarrels and colonial hostility, for extracting perhaps the most liberal concessions from colonial power, and for initiating the quest for national unity."[15]

While Libyan independence in 1951 was a major threshold for the Libyan people, it produced many contradictions. A Libyan state was created without strong Libyan nationhood. Dominated by tribal *shaykhs* and urban notables, the monarchy faced the heavy task of building nationhood and interacting with the international system. Also, this state was one of the poorest in the world with a per capita GNP of $35 and a 90 percent illiteracy rate—one of the highest rates in the world in 1951. The state was dependent on economic aid and rent in exchange for British and American military bases.

Designed by the United Nations as a federal constitutional monarchy with three regional states, a federal government, and three capitals, the political structure of Libya suffered from weak institutions and strong regional interests. The aloof King Idriss lived in Tubruq next to a British military base in eastern Libya and favored his eastern region of Barqa, even though the population of this region made up only 27 percent of the total population of the country while Tripolitania's population was 68 percent and Fezzan, the southern region, 5 percent. The Sanusi monarchy lasted from 1951 until 1969 when a military coup replaced it and declared Libya a republic.

The Libyan Arab Popular and Socialist Jamahiriyya is the official name of the current state of Libya. *Jamahiriyya* refers in Arabic to the state of the masses.[16] A self-declared revolutionary state governed by an organization of popular committees and congresses with a rich, oil-based, rentier economy,[17] the regime is the creation of what most

Libyans call the First of September Revolution. It originated on September 1, 1969 when a group of young pan-Arab, Nassarite officers in the Libyan Royal Army, led by a twenty-seven-year-old charismatic officer named Muammar Abu-Minyar al-Qadhdhafi, overthrew the monarchy of King Muhammad Idriss al-Sanusi in a bloodless coup d'état while the king was vacationing in Turkey. The twelve junior officers were the central committee of a clandestine organization within the Libyan army called the Libyan free unionist officers' movement. The central committee renamed itself the Revolutionary Command Council (RCC) and declared the birth of the Libyan Arab Republic.[18]

The 1969 constitutional proclamation gave the RCC all of the executive, legislative, and judicial powers, and the RCC began to refer to its political and social policies as a revolution. Yet, aside from anticolonialism, anticommunism, Arab nationalism, Islam, and anticorruption, the RCC did not have a clear program of its own and looked to the 1952 Egyptian revolution as a model in the early years. In the last three decades, Libyan society has experienced major social, political, and economic experimentations and transformations. In the absence of popular participation, the new government imposed its social, political, and economic programs on the lower classes. After Qadhdhafi consolidated his power in 1975, he began to experiment with a "precapitalist socialist society," benefiting from the luxury of oil revenues and employing a large non-Libyan expatriate labor force, ironically, the product of Libyan integration in the world capitalist economy.[19]

SOCIAL BASES OF THE REVOLUTION

The radical and nationalist ideology of the Libyan revolution was a reaction to the crisis of the Sanusi monarchy, the persistence of regional identity, and international politics of the last three decades. To summarize, from 1650 to 1911, Libya was known as Tarabulus al-Gharb, a poor and peripheral province of the Ottoman Empire. Although Italy invaded the country in 1911 in one of the most brutal colonial wars in modern Africa, aside from French Algeria and the Belgium Congo, it could not control the hinterland until 1932. Anticolonial resistance was socially based in Ottoman institutions and aid, tribal organizations, and the Islamic ideology of the Sanusi brotherhood. In 1932, when the fascist government in Rome managed to defeat the heroic resistance and conquer the entire country after decimating half of the population (at least a half million people including the educated elite), and pushing another 60,000 Libyans into exile, most Libyans became extremely suspicious of European powers and the West in general. Given this history, RCC members and particularly Qadhdhafi, garnered considerable support by presenting themselves to the Libyan masses as heirs to the anticolonial resistance of the Tripolitanian republic and 'Umar al-Mukhtar.[20]

After discovery and exportation of oil in 1961, the monarchy initiated various programs in health, transportation, housing, and education, including a new Libyan university that opened in 1955 with campuses in Begahazi and Tripoli. By the late 1960s, the educational policies led to the rise of a new salaried middle class, a student movement, a small working class, trade unions, and intellectuals. The Sanusi monarchy depended on Arab teachers from Egypt, Palestine, and Sudan, and they brought with them Arab nationalist ideas to share with their young Libyan students. Most of the first generation of university graduates went to Egyptian universities, and the first class of Libya's military officers graduated from Baghdad Military Academy in Iraq.[21]

By the early 1960s, many young Libyans became involved in Arab nationalist politics of the Nasserite or Baathist branches. The king's aloofness, in turn, aggravated the crisis of the monarchy, which failed to adjust institutionally to its own economic and educational programs. Despite the discovery of oil, many rural Libyans remained poor. As some educated but marginalized middle- and lower-middle-class Libyans found themselves outside the political patronage of old tribal leaders and influential notable families, the military faction of this new middle class became the most organized of the opposition groups and was able to challenge the old elite in 1969.[22]

LIBYA UNDER THE REVOLUTION

The social base of the RCC was predominantly lower-middle class. Only two of the twelve members came from majority tribes, Mhimmad al-Magharif from the Magharba and Abubakr Yunis Jabir from the Majabra. Only one, 'Umar al-Mahashi, came from a prominent family of the coastal city of Misurata (his father was a provincial administrator and from a Circussian Turkish family). The rest came from poor and minor tribes of the interior or the poor social strata of the coastal towns. It could be argued that the revolution was led by a lower-middle class from the interior and the oases against the families from large towns and the dominant tribal leaders.

One of the peculiar policies of the monarchy was its reliance on the police force for its security rather than the army. Numbering 12,000, the police were well-equipped and recruited from loyal tribes, while the small Libyan army never exceeded 6,500. The army drew from the ranks of nonelite students, as did many members of the clandestine free unionist officers' movement and its central committee.[23]

The RCC ideology stressed anticolonialism, Arab nationalism, Islam, self-determination, and social justice. It denounced the corruption of the old regime. RCC officers were also anticommunist, which brought them international recognition from the Nixon administration. Despite claims to radical change, the new regime continued many of the economic and social policies of the monarchy, and continued to develop on a larger scale when the country's infrastructure was built. Most Libyans, in fact, began to benefit from the expanded welfare state with new hospitals, roads, and schools, thanks to increased oil revenues. After successfully negotiating the return of military bases from Britain and the United States, the regime won national support. Further, the regime asserted Libyan control over its oil resources by raising prices and achieving state participation in oil production in 1973, reversing the old regime's policy, which had left the entire oil sector under the control of the multinational oil corporations.[24]

Following the monarchy's policy, the RCC banned political parties and independent trade unions in 1970, and the council adopted the Egyptian model of a one-party system called the Arab Socialist Union in 1971. This model was abandoned two years later when it failed to mobilize the Libyan masses. Facing opposition of the old elite, an apathetic bureaucracy, and the failure of the Arab Socialist Union, Qadhdhafi declared his own popular revolution against the old bureaucracy in the famous speech of Zuwara on July 15, 1973. In the speech he asked the people to replace the old bureaucracy with "popular committees" of employees in their places of work. Qadhdhafi's initiative led to a split within the RCC over the role and authority of the popular committees.[25]

The disagreement reflected major ideological differences inside the RCC over the direction of the revolution. A technocratic faction led by Umar al-Muhashi, the minister of planning, argued the need for expertise and professional competence, while Qadhdhafi insisted on ideological mobilization and political loyalty. When the two factions could not reconcile their differences, the result was a coup inside the RCC led by al-Mahashi against Qadhdhafi. The coup failed when Jallud, a key figure in the council, sided with Qadhdhafi. Umar al-Mahayshi escaped into exile in Tunisia and then Egypt, and Qadhdhafi consolidated his power with four RCC members.[26] By the end of 1975, the ruling Juna of the organization of free officers had lost half of their members due to purges or retirement; the remaining five who sided with Qadhdhafi acted as a cohesive ruling group under Qadhdhafi's leadership. Only five members of the RCC were still in power: Qadh-dhafi, Yunis, Jallud, Kharubi, and Hmaydi. Of the others, Captain Magarif was killed in a car accident; Major Najm was relieved of his duties; Major Garwi fled to the United States; Major Mahashi was later handed back to Qadhdhafi; Major Huni defected to Egypt; and Major Hawadi and Major Hamza were placed under house arrest. Twenty-three free officers were executed after the suppression of the Mahashi coup attempt.

Qadhdhafi began to apply the ideas presented in his *Green Book*, advocating what he called the "Third Universal Theory"—a third approach to merging capitalism and Marxism. The third way called for direct democracy based on popular organization of congresses and committees but simultaneously undermined social and political organizations in the independent trade unions, students' organizations, and the army itself. By 1997, however, when the Libyan Arab Popular and Socialist Jamahir-iyya was officially declared, Qadhdhafi had become impatient with the opposition within the popular committees and the People's General Congress and called for a new organization, the Revolutionary Com-mittees, to instruct and mobilize the popular committees. The new committees were composed of Qadhdhafi loyalists who were indoctri-nated to protect the security of the regime. While many Libyans began leaving the country, most continued to enjoy the benefits of the welfare state and support the government through most of the 1970s.

By the early 1980s, the revolutionary leadership under Qadhdhafi pursued an independent international foreign policy: buying arms from the USSR, supporting liberation movements in Africa and the Middle East such as the Palestinian resistance, and opposing the Amer-ican-sponsored Camp David peace agreement between Egypt and Israel. When President Ronald Reagan was elected, he targeted Qadhdhafi's regime as a sponsor of terrorism and beginning in 1981, attempted to overthrow or weaken the Libyan government by assisting Qadhdhafi's enemies inside and outside of Libya. In 1981, a major American covert action in Chad resulted in defeat of the Libyan army and its Chadian allies.[27]

On April 14, 1986, after a terrorist bomb exploded in a Berlin night-club frequented by American soldiers, the Reagan administration accused Libya of the bombing and authorized an air strike against the country. Despite the fact that these accusations turned out to be false, American jets hit the Libyan cities of Tripoli and Begahazi killing fifty civilians on April 14, 1986.

Facing a hostile regional and international environment and new challenges including American economic sanctions,[28] the regime became isolated in the Arab world. A number of opposition groups were formed in exile, and when oil prices declined drastically in 1986, the regime became very isolated. In 1988, Qadhdhafi blamed the revolutionary committees for abusing their power. He released political prisoners and abandoned much of his experimentation with precapitalist collective markets and bartering.[29]

The collapse of the USSR ended the Cold War in 1989, making the United States the only superpower and the United Nations Security Council another instrument of American foreign policy. The Clinton administration maintained economic sanctions on Libya and in 1992 accused two Libyan nationals of the bombing that led to the 1988 explosion of a Pan-Am plane over Lockerbie, Scotland. When the Qadhdhafi government refused to turn over the suspects, the United States sponsored a United Nations Security Council resolution banning direct flights to Libya and reducing Libyan diplomatic missions abroad. In response, the Qadhdhafi government began to institutionalize power by forming the Ministry of Social Mobilization to replace the revolutionary committees and adopted the regime view of human rights known as the Libyan Green Charter of Human Rights. These measures restored the government to the Arab regional system and prompted resumption of diplomatic ties with other Arab states.

The Libyan revolution brought many positive changes for ordinary Libyans (especially women), including free medical care, a modern infrastructure, and free education, exceeding the achievements of the monarchy. The literacy rate in Libya today is an impressive 75 percent. This is a major achievement in light of the 90 percent illiteracy rate in 1951. No one can deny the existence of a centralized state and the fact that ordinary Libyans are in charge of their own society. At the same time, the Libyan economy is currently more dependent on oil for its revenues than it was under the old regime, and agriculture continues to decline despite large and expensive projects. In 1990, Libyan agriculture contributed only 2 percent to the national budget, and most Libyans are still employed in the state service sector. Once-vibrant institutions and civil associations indicating promise for Libyan society in the 1970s are now either weakened or destroyed.[30] At this stage, an estimated 100,000 Libyans, including some of the best educated, live outside the country.

In 1993 I visited my family in the southern city of Sabha in Fezzan. My old and ill parents were trying to adjust their lives to new economic hardships due to a decline in oil prices and the imposition of economic sanctions. My father retired fifteen years ago after forty years as a teacher and a civil servant—a true community man. Forced to return to work because of the high inflation rate of the Libyan currency, he was finding solace in his deep Islamic faith. My mother needed an operation, but medical care in Sabha and elsewhere in the country is unpredictable, so she decided to wait rather than take a chance; traveling abroad for treatment requires money. Social and cultural associations, such as the Boy Scouts, soccer clubs, and independent student unions are absent. Even the one local movie theater had disappeared along with a sense of hope. I was, however, delighted to see my brothers, sisters, cousins, nieces, and nephews all attending schools or universities. Even in times of insecurity and hardship, life goes on.

CONCLUSION

Recasting the Arab and African state requires a critical reexamination of both Western and nationalist African theories of the state, analyzing the region's history, and exploring alternative perspectives to explain social and political development. Knowledge is often circumstantial and constrained within institutional and social boundaries. Modern social science developed in response to European problems at a point in history when Europe dominated the world. It was inevitable, therefore, that Western social science reflected European choices of subject, theories, categories, and epistemology.

The history of Arab and African societies including Libya in this century has been dominated by colonialism and populist (pre-1940) nationalism. However, since the mid-twentieth century, statist nationalist movements, which led the fight for independence, have assumed state power and produced their own nationalist historiography. While Arab and African nationalist historiography has challenged French, British, Italian, Portuguese, and Spanish colonialism, it still accepts the patterns formulated by colonial scholarship, such as the periodization of history, the model of the nation-state, and the notions of progress and modernity.

The lessons of the Jamahiriyya experiment in Libya are mixed. In terms of both scholarship and the experiment itself, the very idea of building a state based on indigenous institutions and cultural values, and questioning Western hegemony and its definitions of progress and the nation-state are positive contributions. The Jamhiriyya promised to create a cohesive people from a variety of ancient social and regional structures that remained in place as late as the early 1950s. The government, however, faced a paradox: in democratizing its base and educating from the bottom up, the educational system inevitably aimed at homogenizing the culture. Meanwhile, the leadership of the Libyan government failed to encourage the growth of strong institutions or establish accountability and thus weakened associational civic life. More important, the government continues to refuse to learn from its mistakes, viewing criticism as treason or conspiracy. This attitude in turn fosters a brain drain, depriving the government of able professionals to deal with a complex international system. Unless these shortcomings are recognized and other able Libyans are invited to help rebuild the economic, civic, and social institutions, the Jamahiriyya institutions may not outlast Qadhdhafi. In this case, Libya will face the next century without strong institutions, posing a formidable obstacle to its leaders and a terrible hardship on its people.

POSTSCRIPT

Since 1998 the Libyan government has shifted its foreign policy focus from pan-Arabism to pan-Africanism in response to what the Libyan leadership viewed as the Arab states' lack of support for Libya against the sanctions imposed by United States and the United Nations after 1992, and in contrast, as an appreciation of the African states' support and defiance of these sanctions. Many American political commentators concluded this shift to be a new phase of Libyan foreign policy.

But Libyan society has had old and long commercial, ethnic, and religious ties with the sub-Sahara and especially central and west Africa at least since the nineteenth century. In other words, Libya has played an influential rule in African politics since the September revolution of 1969, led by the charismatic Colonel Muammar Qadhdhafi. Prior to an objective assessment of the vital role of Libya in African politics, there is a need for a critical reading of the conventional view of this role in the Western media and mainstream scholarship, where Libyan politics are often demonized and reduced to Qadhdhafi's personality (viewed as irrational and unpredictable) or what became known in the American media as the Mad Dog Syndrome. This image is born of a historical and ideological viewpoint often fixated on Qadhdhafi, and reduces Libya's culture, history, and society to its leader and vice versa. Such a conventional view assumes, as in the colonial period, that the Sahara is an empty space and a divide between the Maghrib and sub-Saharan Africa, and that Libya's role in the rest of Africa is an aberration.

My alternative approach to this topic is to focus on the social bases of Libyan location and history, which linked Libya to the Sahara and the rest of central Sudan through the local states, the trans-Sahara trade, or the heritage of the Sanusiyya movement deeply rooted in the Sahara and Libya in the nineteenth and early twentieth centuries. Furthermore, the September revolution led by Qadhdhafi established strong anticolonial and antiwhite minority regimes in Africa. Finally, the policies of the revolutionary regime in Tripoli were motivated by its own personal and national interests, especially in playing balance-of-power politics against its rivals in Egypt, Israel, Tunisia, Sudan, Algeria, and Morocco. It should not be a big surprise to see the changes in Libyan polices from one stage to another as the balance of power in the region and confrontation with the United States and France in Africa pressured the regime to change its policies or to create alliances or unity agreements with various North African or Saharan states. In short, Libya's politics in Africa have changed due to changing domestic, regional, and international conditions and politics. Since 1996, Libyan policies in Africa have gone through three stages: (1) a period of defiance against colonialism and Israeli influence and support for liberation movements (1969 until 1980); (2) a period of isolation and confrontation with the United States, which led to internal struggle in Libya; and (3) the disastrous defeat in Chad and the American and United Nations sanctions in 1986 and 1992, respectively. During this period, Libyan policies were reactive and supported repressive regimes in Uganda, Liberia, and the Central African Republic. The third stage of Libyan policy is more realistic and positive, after it managed to accept its responsibility for the Lockerbie crisis and after it received African support during the sanction years. The regime accepted the International Court of Justice's ruling on the Aouzo strip dispute with Chad, despite the fact that it lost the case in 1994. It also led the effort to revitalize the Organization of African Unity (OAU) and the creation of the African Union in 2001, mediated many African disputes, and has invested millions in Africa—more than any other state with the exception of South Africa. In short, Libya's mature pan-African policies today may qualify the state to play a constructive and positive role in African disputes, especially if the new realism and reconciliation with the West is applied to domestic politics, such as the rule of law, state building, and empowering civil society.

GLOSSARY

'a'ilat 'a'ilah. — Family, household.

'abd (pl. *'abid*). — Slave.

'agha. — Lord, master; commander of the janissary military troops. In Cyrenaica, an *'agha* is an aid to the head of a religious lodge.

'alim (pl. *'ulama*). — Scholar or specialist on Islamic law.

'atwa (pl. *'atawat*). — Tribute.

'ayan. — A notable.

bait. — House, household.

baraka (pl. *barakat*). — God's blessing; a person who is blessed with *baraka* is called *murabit* or *sharif.*

bay'a. — An oath of fealty; homage, consent.

Bilad al-Maghrib. — From Arabic, the western region of the Arab Muslim world from Libya to Morocco.

Bilad al-Sudan. — Literally, the land of the blacks; the name given by Arabs to the region south of the Sahara and between the Nile and the Atlantic Ocean prior to European colonialism.

Cologhli or Kolughli. — From Turkish Kolughlu; descendants of intermarriage between Turkish troops and local North African women.

dalu or dalaw. — Goatskin water container drawn up by a donkey and guided and labored by a peasant, who is called a *jabbad* in southern Libya.

dariba (pl. *dara'ib*). — Tax.

dhikr (pl. *'adhkar*). — Sufi term for chanting and repetition of certain words or poems in praise of God.

din. — Religion.

duwr (pl. *'adwar*). — Division, turn; a division of anticolonial tribal resistance in Libya during the colonial period.

fallah or fellah (pl. *fallahin* or *fellahin*). — Peasant.

fatha or fatiha. — Start; the opening of each chapter of the Quran; prayer to gain the help or the blessing of God.

fatwa (pl. *fatawa* and *fatawi*). — Formal legal opinion given by an *'alim* or jurist of standing to a question posed to him by a judge or individual.

ferman or **faraman**. — Ottoman imperial decree, edict, letter of commission or appointment.

habs or **habus** (pl. *hubus*). — North African term for *waqf* or religious endowment.

hadith. — Reported words and deeds of the prophet Muhammad by a reliable chain of transmitters and scholars of Islamic law. The Quran and the *hadith* constitute the major authoritative sources of Islamic law.

hamada. — Stony desert plateau; among the largest in Libya is hamada al-Hamra, located between southern Tripolitania and northern Fezzan.

ijaza. — Graduation certificate for outstanding students of Islamic law.

ijtihad. — Scholarly free interpretation of Islamic law by qualified scholar of standing. The conventional view is that *ijtihad* was closed by the twentieth century and *taqlid*, or conformity, was accepted in Islamic law. This static view has been challenged, as many scholars pointed out that even if conservative *'ulama* closed the gates of *ijtihad*, people still reinterpret the law in new ways.

ikhwan. — Brothers, brethren, members of a religious order.

iltizam. — Tax concession on agriculture.

imam. — Leader of prayers attached to a mosque; leader of the community or the state in Shii and Kharaiji Islam.

jabal. — Mountain.

jabbad. — Peasant hired to irrigate the farm of a landlord in exchange for a share of the crop according to an initial agreement. The sharecropper, *jabbad*, draws water from a well using a donkey.

Jamahiriyya. — From Arabic, the state of the masses; the official name of Libya after 1977.

janissary. — Ottoman military corps until the beginning of the nineteenth century.

jaziya. — Tax levied on non-Muslims living under Muslim rule.

jihad. — Religious struggle against inner base impulses and desires, and also against the infidels who threaten the land of Islam.

khalifa (pl. *khulafa*). — Caliph, successor of the prophet, title of the ruler of the Muslim state.

khammas (pl. *khammasa*). — Sharecropper in North Africa, often receives a fifth of the harvest in exchange for his labor.

lahma. — In western Libya, refers to clan or subtribe.

magharssa. — Contract between a sharecropper and landowner in North Africa. The sharecropper agrees to plant and irrigate palm and olive trees in exchange for a share of these trees by the time of the first harvest.

mahalla. — State military expedition or camp to subdue a rebellion and collect tributes in nineteenth-century North Africa.

miriland. — State land.

mithiqal. — Weight, currency unit of gold.

mtalian or **talian** (pl. *mutalinin*). — "Gone Italian"; *harqi* in Algeria, a term used in Libya to describe Libyans who collaborated with the Italian colonial state as soldiers and bureaucrats.

mu'alim (pl. *mu'alimin*). — Teacher.

mudir. — Administrator of a subdistrict or *nahiya*.

mufti. — Scholar of outstanding knowledge in religious matters who gives formal legal opinion, or *fatwa*, to questions posed to him by a judge.

mujahid (pl. *mujahidin*). — Fighter against infidels. *See* **jihad.**

mulk. — Property, private property.

muqadm. — Foreman, military officer, head of a religious lodge.

murabit (pl. *murabtin*). — Saint; individual who has *baraka*; client tribesmen in Cyrenaica.

mu'taqalat. — Concentration camps.

mutasarrif. — Provincial governor of a district, or *mutasarrifiyya*, in Ottoman Libya in the second half of the nineteenth century.

pasha. — Governor-general of a province, or *wilayat*; big landlord, high military or ministerial person in the Ottoman Empire. The governor of Ottoman Libya in Tripoli was called *pasha*. The rules of the independent Qaramanli state retained the title of *pasha* from 1711 to 1835.

Porte. — The office of grand vizier in Istanbul, the highest political office in the Ottoman Empire.

qabila (pl. *qaba'il*). — Tribe.

qadi or **kadi.** — Judge.

qaimmaqam. — Administrator of a district or *qaimmaqamiyya* in Ottoman Libya in the second half of the nineteenth century.

Quraish. — Prophet Muhammad's tribe; one of the most powerful tribes in seventh-century Arabia, which controlled the city of Mecca. Muslims have always accorded respect to the descendants of Quraish. Some Muslim jurists even required Quraishi kinship as a qualification for leadership of the Muslim community.

Quran or **Koran.** — The written words of Allah as revealed through the prophet Muhammad; Muslim holy book.

Sa'adi. — From Sa'da, the ancestress of the ten Sa'adi tribes of Cyrenaica. These tribes were members of the Arab Hilali conquering tribes of North Africa in the eleventh century. Hence they have owned most of the fertile land and water resources at the expense of early Arab and Berber Murabtin tribes in Cyrenaica. These ten tribes are 'Abid, 'Urufa, 'Awagir', Magharba, 'Abadydat, Hasa, 'Aylat, Faid, Drasa, and Bra'sa.

sadaqa (pl. *sadaqat*). — Alms, voluntary contribution of alms for the sake of God's rewards.

sagai. — Water carrier, sharecropper, peasant who is hired to irrigate a land-owner's farm in exchange for a percentage of the harvest or a salary in North Africa.

saniya (pl. *swani*). — Well; farm in North Africa.

shabardag. — Barbed wire, concentration camps in eastern Libyan Arabic.

shari'a — Law, Islamic law; includes the Quran, the deeds and the statements of prophet Muhammad, the consensus of the Muslim community, and the reasoning of the *ulama*.

sharif (pl. *asfraf* or *shurufa*). — A noble; a person who is believed to descend from the prophet's family through his daughter Fatima.

shaykh or **shaikh.** — Elder, dignitary, leader of prayers at a mosque, *'alim*, tribal chief.

shwashna. — Descendants of freed black slaves in North Africa.

sidi or **sayyid** (pl. *sadah* or *assyad*). — Colloquial from *Sayyidi*, Sir; respected person of status from *sharif* or *murabitic* background in North Africa.

suff (pl. *sufuf*). — Line, tribal confederation and alliance in southern Tunisia, Tripolitania and Fezzan in Libya during the nineteenth century.

Sufi. — Mystic; a major trend in Islam that stresses the inner spiritual experience. In North Africa, Sufi Islam dominated popular culture from the fourteenth century.

sultan. — Title of a ruler, the ruler of the Ottoman Empire.

sunna. — The deeds and statements of the prophet Muhammad as accepted by a reliable chain of transmitters. Muslims who believe in the Sunna are called *Sunni*.

takhris. — Process of estimating the harvest of olive or palm trees by state tax collectors in nineteenth-century Ottoman Libya.

tanzimat. — Literally, in Turkish, "beneficent legislation"; Ottoman reforms from 1839 to 1876.

tariqa (pl. *turaq*). — Path, religious Sufi order.

'umma. — Islamic community.

'ushr (pl. *'ashar*). — Tithe, ten percent tax on agricultural produce also known as *zakat*; one of the five pillars of Islam.

wabbar. — Person who fertilizes palm trees in Fezzan.

wadi (pl. *'awdiya* or *widiyan*). — Valley.

wald (pl. *'awlad*). — Child, boy, descendant (e.g., Awlad Sulayman).

wali (pl. *wulat*). — Provincial governor of *wilayat* in the Ottoman Empire.

walii (pl. *'awliya*). — Saint, *murabit* who is believed to have *baraka* in North Africa. After the death of a *walii*, his tomb or lodge becomes a shrine and a place of sanctity.

waqf. — Religious endowment. *See* **habs.**

watan. — Homeland.

wilayat. — In Turkish, *iyala* and *vilayet*; province of the Ottoman Empire. A *wilayat* is made of a district, *mutasarrifiyya*, a subdistrict, *qaimmaqamiyya*, and a sub-subdistrict, a *mudiriyya* or *nahiya*. This was the administrative system of the Ottoman Empire during the second half of the nineteenth century.

zakat. — Alms. *See* **'ushr.**

zawiya (pl. *zawayya*). — Lodge, mosque, hospice, or school complex of a religious Sufi order (e.g., the Sanusiyya).

NOTES

Introduction

1. Eric Hobsbawm, *Nations and Nationalism since 1780*, (Cambridge: Cambridge University Press, 1990) and David Held, "The Decline of the Nation-State," in *Becoming National: A Reader*, eds. Geof Eley and Ronald Grigor Suny (Oxford: Oxford University Press, 1996), 407–17.

2. On the impact of colonialism, world system, and Eurocentrism, see Edward Said, *Culture and Imperialism* (New York: Vintage Books, 1993); Immanuel Wallerstein, "Open the Social Sciences," *Items: Social Science Research Council* 50, no. 1 (March 1996): 1–7; and Eric Wolf, *Europe and the People without History* (Berkeley: University of California Press, 1982). On the concept of power, see Steven Lukes, *Power: A Radical View* (London: Macmillan, 1974), 23; and Michel Foucault, "Lecture Two," in *Culture/Power/History: A Reader in Contemporary Social Theory*, eds. Nicholas B. Dirks, Geoff Eley, and Sherry B. Ortner (Princeton, NJ: Princeton University Press, 1994), 210–11. On the concept of agency, see Ibn Khaldun, *The Muqaddimah: An Introduction to History* (Princeton, NJ: Princeton University Press, 1967); E. P. Thompson, *The Making of the English Working Class* (New York: Vintage Books, 1966), 11; and James Scott, *Weapons of the Weak* (New Haven, CT: Yale University Press, 1985), and his other book *Domination and the Arts of Resistance: Hidden Transcripts* (New Haven, CT: Yale University Press, 1990) especially chapters 1 and 8.

Chapter 1

1. An example for dynastic history is Tahir Ahmad al-Zawi's *Wulat Tarabulus al-Gharb Min bidayat al-Fath al Ararabi ila nihayat al-Ahd al-Turki* (The governors of Tripoli from the beginning of the Arab conquest until the end of the Turkish era) (Beirut: Dar al-Fatah Lil Nishir, 1970). For modernization theory, see Abdullah Ali Ibrahim, "Evolution of Government and Society in Tripolitania and Cyrenaica—Libya, 1935" (Ph.D. diss., University of Utah, 1982); and Lisa S. Anderson, "States, Peasants and Tribes: Colonialism and Rural Politics in Tunisia and Libya" (Ph.D. diss., Columbia University, 1981).

2. Ibrahim Ahmad Rizqanah *al-Mamulakah al-Libiyah* (The Libyan Monarchy) (Cairo: Dar al-Nahdah al-'Arabiyah, 1964) 32, 39, 73.

3. On the Hilali conquest, see J. Poncet, "Le Mythe de La Catastrophe Hilalienne," *Annales Economics Societies, Civilizations* XXII (1967): 1097–1120; Radi Daghfus, "al-Awamil al-Iqtisadiya Li-hijarat Bani Hilal wa Bani Salim Ila Afriqiyah"

(the Economic Factors behind the Migration of Ban Hilal and Salim to North Africa), in *Awraq* (Madrid, April, 1981) 147–63; and a good summary of the debate over the impact of nomadism in Rhoads Murphy's essay "The Decline of North Africa since the Roman Occupation: Climate or Human?" *Association of American Geographers* 41 (June 1951): 116–32.

4. Drought hit the regency in 1856, 1859, 1881–82, and 1901–3.
5. Adu A. Boahen, "The Caravan Trade in the Nineteenth Century," *Journal of African History* 111, no. 2 (1972): 350; and Dennis D. Cordell, "Eastern Libya Wadai and the Sanusiyya: Atarigo and a Trade Route," *Journal of African History* 18, no. 2 (1972): 25.
6. Cordell, 25.
7. Ahmad Said al-Fituri, "Tripolitania, Cyrenaica, and Bilad As-Sudan: Trade Relations during the Second Half of the Nineteenth Century" (Ph.D. diss., University of Michigan, 1982), 45–56.
8. In 1911, the city of Tripoli's population was 29,664. For the role of the city as a commercial and urban market, see Robert Harrison, "Migrants in the City of Tripoli," *Geographical Journal* 57 (July 1967): 406.
9. For example, Ghadamis had a population of 12,000 in 1804, which declined to 6,831 in 1911 and 3,000 in 1965; Murzaq had a population of 5,000 in 1867, which declined to just 1,000 in 1911.
10. Until now there has been no major study of this Libyan Saharan state. What we know comes from descriptions by the Libyan historian Ibn Ghalbun and some European travelers (e.g., Hornemann, 1789; Barth, 1849; and Nachtigal, 1869). An important source was recently discovered: a manuscript by an unknown writer, which was copied by the Tripolitanian notable al-Khuja, is called *Tarikh Fezzan*, ed. Habib Wadaa al-Hisnawi (Tripoli: Center for Libyan Studies, 1979).
11. Paolo Della Cella, *Narrative of an Expedition from Tripoli in Barbary to the Western Frontier of Egypt in 1817 by the Bey of Tripoli*, trans. Anthony Aufrere (London: John and Arthur Arch, 1822), 194; and the notes of British traveler James Hamilton, *Wanderings in North Africa* (London: John Murry, Albemarie, 1856), 9, 56.
12. Ahmad Abuzied, "The Sedentarization of Nomads in the Western Desert of Egypt," *International Social Science Journal* X, no. 4 (1959): 550; and E. E. Evans-Pritchard, *The Sanusi of Cyrenaica* (Oxford: Oxford University Press, 1949), 44, 46.
13. Evans-Pritchard, *The Sanusi*, 10–11, 18, 69, 71.
14. Muhammed Khalil Ibn Ghalbun, *al-Tidhkar Fiman Malaka Tarabulus Wa Makana Biha Min Akhbr* (A reminder of Tripoli's rulers and her history), 2nd ed., ed. T. A. al-Zawi (Tripoli: Maktabat al-nur, 1967), 158.
15. See the script of three tribes in 'Umar Ibn Isma'il, *Inhiyar Hukm al-Usrah al-Qaramanliyah Fi Libya 1795–1835* (The Collapse of the Qaramanli Dynasty in Libya) (Tripoli: Maktabat al-Firjani, 1866), 448–52, 478–79.
16. Hasan al-Faqih Hasan, *Al-yawmiyat al Libiyya* (The Libyan Daily) Part 1 (1551–1832), eds. Muhammad al-Usta and 'Amar Jhaydir (Tripoli: Center for Libyan Studies, 198), 599; and Ahmad al-Naib al-Ansari, *Al-Manhal al-Adhb Fi Tarikh Tarabulus al Gharb* (The sweet source for the history of Tripoli of the west) (Tripoli: Maktabat al Firjani), 235. The debt of Yusuf Qaramanli was estimated to be $500,000 according to the French counsel Charles Feraud, *Annales Tripolitanes* (Paris: Librairie Vaibert, 1927), 363.
17. Al-Ansari, *Al-Mauhal*, 14–15; and Seton Deardon, *A Nest of Corsairs* (London: John Murry, 1976), 299–342.
18. LNA (Libyan National Archives), Malaf al-Aradi, land tenure file.
19. On Libyan peasantry, see Adolf Vischer, "Tripoli," *Geographical Journal* XXXVII, no. 5 (November 1911): 487–88; and Jean Despois, "Types of Native Life in Tripolitania,"

Geographical Review 35 (1944–1945); Alger: Institut de Recherches Sahariennes de L'Universite D'Alger (Paris, 1946), 29, 63.

20. Perry Anderson, *Passages from Antiquity to Feudalism* (London: Newlef Review, 1974), 217–28.

21. Yusuf Toni, "Tribal Distribution and Racial Relationships of the Ancient and Modern Peoples of Cyrenaica," Jami'at Ayn Shams. Kulliyat al-Adab, *Hawliyal Kulliyat al-Adab* (1963), 172.

22. For an overview of tribal political confederation, see 'Umar Said Baghni, "Asul Harakat al Sufuf wa A tharuha ala Harakat al-Jihad al-Libi" (The genesis of Sufuf and its impact on Libyan Jihad), *Al-Shahid* 4 (1983): 97.

23. See Lisa Anderson, "Nineteenth Century Reform in Ottoman Libya," *International Journal of Middle East Studies*, 16 (1984): 325–48.

24. See Allen Streicker, "Government and Revolt in Tripoli Regency, 1795–1855" (Master's thesis, Northwestern University, 1970); and Ibrahim, "The Rebellious Movement against the Ottomans 1835–58" in "The Evolution of Government" (see n. 1), 79–118.

25. E. G. H. Joffe, "British Molta and the Qaramanli Dynasty 1800–1835," *Revue D'Histoire Maghrebine*, 12 eme Annes: 37–38 (January 1985): 32.

26. Tripolitanian Esparto, Ports to England began in 1885; 20,000 tons grew to a peak of 210,000 tons in 1888, but declined by 1905 to 99,000 tons. See Great Britain Public Record Office n 3919, Session 1908, Vol. 116.

27. Harrison, "Migrants to the City of Tripoli," 415.

28. Fituri, "Tripolitania," 84.

29. Despois, *Geographie Humaine*, 182, and by the same author, *Le Djebal ne Fousa* (Triolitainei) (Paris: Etude Geographique, 1935), 166–67. During the 1920s, around 20,000 Libyans lived in Tunisia.

30. See Muhammad Naji and Muhammad Nuri, *Tarabulus al-Gharb*, (Tripoli: Dar Maktabat al-Fikir, 1973), 70–1

31. The Bank of Rome had a budget of $5 million lira. It began investing in Libya in 1907, mainly in land and agriculture (oil and esparto factories), and built four mills and one ice factory. See R. Mori, "La Penetrationi Pacifica Italiana in Libia dal 1907 al 1911 eil Banco di Roma," *Revista di Studi Politici Internationali*, 24 (1957): 110–11.

32. For example, the mayor of Tripoli, Hassuna Qaramanli, the merchant 'Umar al-Muntasir, and Jewish merchants. These notables bought land for the bank and later, after 1911, collaborated with colonial administration; they had contact with the Italian government beginning in the 1880s. See Francesco Crispi, *The Memoirs of Francesco Crispi*, vol. II, ed. Thomas Palamenghi-Crispi, trans. Mary Prichard-Agnetti (London: Hodder and Stroughton, 1912), 474–475.

33. In 1798 Horrenmann estimated the population of Fezzan around 75,000, Nachtigal in 1869 estimated the number to be 50,000, and De Agostini, in 1917, recorded Fezzan's population to be just 31,600.

34. Despois, *Geographie Humaine*, 182–83.

35. The best political history of the Sanusiyya is Ahmad Sidqi al-Dajani, *al-Harakah al-Sanusiyya*, 2nd. ed. (Cairo: al-Matba'al-Faniyya, 1988), but no attempt, to our knowledge, has been made to study the political economy of the region and its impact on the Sanusiyya.

36. Nicola Ziadeh, *Sanusiyah: A Study of a Revivalist Movement* (Leiden: Brill, 1958), 48.

37. Evans-Pritchard estimated the number of Sanusi Lodges to be 146 in the 1920s. *The Sanusi*, 24.

38. For a discussion of the process of class formation (e.g., *peasantization*), see Ken Post, "Peasantization" and "Rural Political Movements in Western Africa," *Archives Europeennes de Sociologie* XIII, no. 2 (1972): 226–27. For an analysis of peasantization and

proletarianization, see Salim Tamari, "Factionalism and Class Formation in Recent Palestinian History," in *Studies in the Economic and Social History of Palestine in the Nineteenth and Twentieth Centuries*, ed. Roger Owen (Oxford: St. Anthony's College, 1982), 193–99.

39.   On the population of Ghadamis, see 'Imad Ghanim, *Al-Fusul al-Arba'ah* (April 1979); on Murzaq and Ghat, see Francesco Coro, *Settantessei Anni di Mominizione Turca in Libia, 1935–1911* (Tripoli: Dar al-Firjani, 1971), 134, 149; and De Agostini, *Populazioni Della Tripolitania*, 202. The best study of these oases is still found in Lars Eldblom, *Structure Fonciere Organizationel Structure Social* (unickol-Lund, 1968).

Chapter 2

1.   For an overview of the Ottoman Iberian conflict in North Africa, see Andrew C. Hess, *The Forgotten Iberian African Frontiers* (Chicago, IL: University of Chicago Press, 1978).

2.   For an introduction to the geography and the ecology of the Fezzan, see Ibrahim Rizqara, *al-Mamalaka al-Libiyya* (The Libyan Kingdom) (Cairo: Dar al-Nahda al-Arabiyya, 1964), and J. Lethielleux, *Le Fezzan: Ses Jardins es ses Palmiers* (Tunis: Imprimerie Bascone & Muscat, 1949).

3.   See Habib Wadaa El-Hisnawi, *Fezzan under the Rule of the Awlad Muhammad: A Study in Political, Economic, and Social and Intellectual History* (Sebha: Center for African Researches and Studies, 1990), 36–61.

4.   Muhammed Khalil Ibn Ghalbun, *al-Tidhkar Fiman Malaka Tarabulus Wa Makana Biha Min Akhbr* (A reminder of Tripoli's rulers and her history), 2nd. ed., ed. T. A. al-Zawi (Tripoli: Maktabat al-nur, 1967), 125–26.

5.   Wabib Wadaa El-Hisnawi, ed., *Watha'iq Dawlat Awlad Muhammad* (Documents of the State of Awlad Muhammad), vol. 1 (Tripoli: Center for Libyan Studies, 1994).

6.   The most detailed study of the state of Awlad Muhammad is El-Hishnawi's *Fezzan under the State of Awlad Muhammad* (see n. 3 above).

7.   F. Hornemann, "The Journal of F. Hornemann's Travels from Cairo to Marzuk in the Years 1797–98," in *Missions to the Niger*, ed. E. W. B. Bovil (Cambridge: Cambridge University Press, 1969), 102.

8.   G. Nathtigal, *Sahara and the Sudan, Tripoli and Fezzan*, vol. I, trans. B. B. Fisher and Humphery G. Fisher (New York: Barnes & Noble, 1974), 87, 122.

9.   See 'Umar Ibn Isma'il, *Inhiyar Hukm al-Usrah al-Qaramanliyah Fi Libya 1795–1835* (The Collapse of the Qaramanli Dynasty in Libya) (Tripoli: Maktabat al-Firjani, 1866), 448–52, 478–79.

10.   Unkown author, *Tarikh Fezzan*, ed. Habib Wadaa al-Hisnawi (Tripoli: Center for Libyan Studies, 1979), 57; and Hornemann, "Journal," 100.

11.   The best scholarly works on the Qaramanli state under Yusuf Pasha are Ben Ishma'il, *Inhiyar* (in Arabic) and Kola Folayan, *Tripoli under the Reign of Yusuf Pasha Qaramanli* (IFE, Nigeria: University of IFE Press, 1975).

12.   Ibn Ghalbun, *al-Tidhkar*, 153 and *Tarikh Fezzan*, 67

13.   Ibn Ghalbun, *al-Tidhkar*, 158.

14.   Ibn Ishma'il, *Inhiyar*, 230.

Chapter 3

1.   I am referring here primarily to the segmentary model of analysis as articulated by British social anthropologists, particularly E. E. Evans-Pritchard and Ernest Gellner, and to the work of modernization theorists such as Daniel Lerner. See the classic work by Evans-Pritchard, *The Sanusi of Cyrenaica* (Oxford: Clarendon Press, 1949),

59–60; and Gellner's *Saints of the Atlas* (Chicago, IL: University of Chicago, 1969), 35–70. Critiques of this model include David Seddon, "Economic Anthropology or Political Economy: Approaches to the Analysis of Pre-Capitalist Formation in the Maghrib," in *The New Economic Anthropology*, ed. John Clamer (London: Macmillan, 1978), 61–107; Talal Asad, "The Idea of an Anthropology of Islam (Washington, D.C.: Georgetown University Center for Contemporary Arab Studies, 1968), 8–11; Lila Abu-Lughod, "Zones of the Theory in the Anthropology of the Arab World," *Annual Review of Anthropology* 18 (1989): 280–87.

Works informed by modernization methodologies include Daniel Lerner's *The Passing of Traditional Society: Modernization in the Middle East* (New York: Free Press, 1958), 47; and Lisa Anderson, *The State and Social Transformation in Tunisia and Libya, 1830–1980* (Princeton, NJ: Princeton University Press, 1986). Anderson gives information on Libyan social history not previously available in the English language, but her reliance on modernization methodology leads her to view social change as coming from the modernizing states that ruled Libya, either Ottoman or Italian; she thus fails to address nineteenth-century Ottoman Libya's complex social and economic structure. For more details, see my review of this book published in the *Arab Journal of International Studies* 1, no. 2 (summer 1988): 110–15. Greater details on this and other issues discussed in this chapter are available in my book *The Making of Modern Libya: State Formation, Colonization, and Resistance, 1830–1932* (Albany: State University of New York Press, 1994).

2. On the state increasing its presence by building a modern network of telegraph communication, see A. S. Dajani and 'A. S. Ad'ham, *Watha'iq tarikh Libiya al-hadith: al-watha'iq al-'Uthmaniyah, 1881–1911* (Benghazi: University of Benghazi Press, 1974), 169.

3. Michel F. Le Gall, "Pashas, Bedouins, and Notables in the Ottoman Administration in Tripolitania and Benghazi, 1881–1902" (Ph.D. diss., Princeton University, 1986), 117.

4. E. L. Peters, "Cultural and Social Diversity," in *Libya since Independence: Economic and Political Development*, ed. A. J. Allan (New York: St. Martins Press, 1982), 106.

5. B. Yusha, *Ghadamis, watha'iq tijariyah tarikyiyah ijtima'iyah (1228–1310 Hijri)* (Tripoli: Libyan Studies Center, 1982), 109; and D. Cordell, "The Awlad Sulayman of Libya and Chad: Power and Adaptation in the Sahara and Sahel," *Canadian Journal of African Studies* 19, no. 2 (1985): 330.

6. G. Nachtigal, *Sahara and Sudan*, vol. 1 (New York: Barnes & Noble, 1974), 122; F. Coro, *Settantasei anni di dominazione turca in Libia, 1835–1911* (Tripoli: Dar al-Ferjani, 1971); and E. Rossi, *Storia di Tripoli e della Tripolitania dalla conquista araba al 1911* (Beirut: Dar al-Thaqafa, 1974), 416.

7. On tribesmen and peasant migrations to French Tunisia, see J. Despois, *Geografie Humaine* (Algiers: Imbert, 1946), 182–83, and his *Le Djebal Nefousa (Tripolitaine): Étude Geografique* (Paris: Larose, 1935), 166–67; also J. Hilal, "Agriculture and Socio-economic Change in the Region of Misallata, Tripolitania," *Dirassat: Libyan Economic and Business Review* 5 (Benghazi University), no. 1 (1969): 124. On migrations to urban Tripolitania, see R. Harrison, "Migrants in the City of Tripoli," *Geographical Journal* 57 (1967): 415; and A. S. Dajani, *Libya qubayla al-ihtilal al-itali* (Cairo: Al-Matba'a al-Faniyya, 1971), 222, 224, 238.

8. Le Gall, "Pashas," 93.

9. K. Post, "Peasantization and Rural Political Movements in West Africa," *Archives europeenes de sociologie* 8, no. 2 (1972): 229.

10. J. A. N. Brehony, "Seminomadism in the Jabal Tarhune," in *Field Studies in Libya*, eds. S. G. Willimott and J. I. Clarke, (Department of Geography, Durham Colleges in the University of Durham, 1960), 63

11. 'U. A. Ibn Isma'il, *Inhiyar Hukim al-Usra al-Qaramanliya fi Libya (1790–1835)* (Tripoli: Al-Ferjani, 1966), and M. A. al-Twair, "al-Zira'ah fi waliyat tarabulus al-gharb 'athn'a al-hukum al 'uthmani al-mubashir laha, 1835–1911," *Revue d'Histoire Maghrebine* 12 (1985): 39–40, 515–16.
12. Le Gall, "Pashas," 93.
13. On the role of Jewish merchants, see R. Simon, "The Socio-Economic Role of the Tripolitanian Jews in the Late Ottoman Period," in *Communautes juives des marges sahariennes du Maghreb*, ed. M. Abitbol (Jerusalem: Ben-Zvi, 1982), 321–28. On Maltese merchants, see E. G. H. Joffe, "Trade and Migration between Malta and the Barbary States 1835–1911" in M. M. Buru et al., *Planning and Development in Modern Libya* (London: Middle East and North Africa Press, 1985), and his "British Malta and the Qaramanli Dynasty (1800–1835)," *Revue d'histoire maghrebine* 12: Annee: 37–38 (January 1985): 32.
14. A. J. Cachia, *Libya under the Second Ottoman Occupation, 1835–1911* (Tripoli: Government Press, 1945), 1021; Dajani and Ad'ham, *Wathaiq*, 296–98.
15. A. M. al-Misurati, *Sahafat Libya fi nisf garn* (Beirut: Dar al-Kashaf, 1960), 18; also the classic essay by A. Hourani on the role of the *'ayan* in the Ottoman Empire, "Ottoman Reforms and the Politics of the Notables," in *The Beginnings of Modernization in the Middle East: The Nineteenth Century*, eds. W. Falk and R. Chambers (Chicago, IL: University of Chicago Press, 1968), 41–68.
16. Abdul Mola S. El-Horeir, "Social and Economic Transformation in the Libyan Hinterland during the Second Half of the Nineteenth Century: The Role of Sayyid Ahmad Al-Sharif" (Ph.D. diss., University of California, Los Angeles, 1981), 95.
17. Evans-Pritchard, *The Sanusi of Cyrenaica*, 81–82; C. C. Adams, "The Sanusis," *Muslim World* 36, no. 1 (1946): 32.
18. See reports of two British journalists: E. N. Bennett, *With the Turks in Tripoli: Being Some Experiences in the Turco-Italian War of 1911* (London: Methuen, 1912), 186; and Francis McCullagh, *Italy's War for a Desert: Being Some Experiences of a War-Correspondent with the Italians in Tripoli* (Chicago, IL: F. G. Browne, 1913), 18.
19. McCullagh, *Italy's War*, 3; and C. Lapworth and H. Zimmern, *Tripoli and Young Italy* (London: Swift, 1912), 85.
20. G. Giolitti, *Memoirs of My Life* (New York: Howard Fertig, 1973), 260, 279.
21. T. Irace, *With the Italians in Tripoli* (London: J. Murray, 1912), 20.
22. See D. M. T. (Dar al-Mahfuzat al-Tarikhiyya), "Malf al 'A'ilat al-Libiya" [files of Libyan notable families] (Libyan National Archives in Tripoli), 188.
23. M. M. Fushaykah, *Ramadan al-suwayhili: al-batal al-Libi al-shahir bi-kifahihi lil-talyan: wa-fi al-kitab majmu'ah min al-suwar al-tarikhiyah* (Tripoli: Al-Ferjani, 1974), 29–33.
24. Fushaykah, *Ramadan*, 112.
25. See Ahmad Dia al-Din al-Muntasir's letter to S. al-Baruni, in *Safahat Khalida min al jihad*, ed. Z. Al-Baruni (Cairo: Matabi' al-istiqlal al-kubra, 1964), 149–50.
26. E. De Leone, *La Colonizzazione Dell' Africa Del Nord (Algeria, Tunisia, Marocco, Libia)* (Padua: CEDAM, 1957), 390–91, 420; A. M. Barbar, "The Tarabulus (Libyan) Resistance to the Italian Invasion: 1911–1920" (Ph.D. diss., Department of History, University of Wisconsin, Madison, 1980), 266.
27. T. A. al-Zawi, *Jihad al-Abtal fi Tarabulus al-Gharb* (Beirut: Dar al-Fatah lil-Nashir, 1970 [1950]), 118.
28. R. Simon, "The Socio-Economic Role of the Tripolitanian Jews," 324.
29. R. De Felice, *Jews in an Arab Land: Libya, 1835–1970* (Austin: University of Texas Press, 1985), 28, 40.

30. Rosabla Davico, "La Guerrilla Libyenne 1911–1932," in *Abd el-Karim et la Republique du Rif* (Paris: Maspero, 1976), 434–35; Rachel Simon, *Libya between Ottomanism and Nationalism*, (Berlin: Klaw Schwarz Verlag, 1987), 188.
31. T. A. al-Zawi, *Jihad*, 266–67; Rodolfo Graziani, *Cirenaica Pacificata*, (Beghazi: Dar al-Andalus, 1974), 89.

Chapter 4

1. For a critical review of the field, see Ruth Ben-Ghiat, "A Lesser Evil? Italian Fascism in the Totalitarian Equation," in *The Lesser Evil: Moral Approaches to Genocide*, eds. Helmut Dubiel and Gabriel Motzkin (New York: Routledge, 2004), 137–53; Adrian Lyttelton, "What Is Fascism?" *The New York Review of Books*, October 21, 2004, 33–36; and R. J. B. Bosworth, *Italian Dictatorship* (London: Arnold, 1998), 3–4.
2. John P. Diggins, *Mussolini and Fascism: The View from America* (Princeton, NJ: Princeton University Press, 1972), 6.
3. Diggins, 241.
4. Gregory Dale Black, "The United States and Italy 1943–1946: The Drift toward Containment" (Ph.D. diss., University of Kansas, 1973), 13–14.
5. On Italian historiography, see Peter Gran, *Beyond Eurocentrism: A New World View of Modern History* (Syracuse, NY: Syracuse University Press, 1996), 88–121. Also on Italian orientalism, see Anna Baldinetti, *Orientalismo e Colonialismo La ricerca di cousenso in Egitto Per L'impesadi Libia* (Roma: Insititutio per L'oriente "C. A. Nallino," 1997).
6. Diggins, 243; Stanley Kauffmann, "Under Florentine Skies," *New Republic* 2 220, no. 23 (June 7, 1999): 30.
7. Alan Cowell, "The Ghost of Mussolini Keeps Rattling His Chains," *New York Times*, June 1, 1994, 3; James O. Jackson, "Fascism Lives," *Time*, June 6, 1994; and Ian Fisher, "New Italian Minister Sheds Far-Right Image," *New York Times*, November 19, 2004. For a sympathetic view of fascism, see Renzo DeFelice, *Interpretations of Fascism* (Cambridge: Harvard University Press, 1977). On the historiography of Nazism, see Ian Kershaw, *The Nazi Dictatorship* (London: Edward Arnold, 1993).
8. "Duce with the Laughing Face," *People*, April 27, 1992, 70.
9. Hannah Arendt, *Eichman in Jerusalem* (London: Penguin Books, 1994), 178–80, and her other book, *The Origins of Totalitarianism* (New York: Harcourt, Brace and Jovanovich, 1973), 2, 5, 7, 8.
10. Victoria de Grazia, "Will Il Duce's Successors Make the Facts Run on Time?" *New York Times*, May 14, 1994, 21.
11. For a critique of Eurocentrism, see Samir Amin, *Eurocentrism* (New York: Monthly Review Press, 1980). Carl Levy recently wrote a comprehensive review of the comparative analysis of fascist movements still centered on Europe: "Fascism, National Socialism and Conservatives in Europe, 1914–1945," *Contemporary European History* 8, no. 1 (1999): 97–126.
12. See David Forgacs, ed., *The Antonio Gramsci Reader* (New York: New York University Press, 2000), 112–13, 149.
13. Frantz Fanon, *The Wretched of the Earth* (London: Penguin, 1967), 75; and Aimè Ceasaire, *Discourses on Colonialism* (New York: Pantheon, 1988), 12.
14. Mahmood Mamdani, *Good Muslim, Bad Muslim* (New York: Pantheon Books, 2004), 7.
15. See my book, *The Making of Modern Libya: State Formation, Colonization, and Resistance, 1830–1932* (Albany: State University of New York Press, 1994), 135.
16. An early analytical analysis of the brutal fascist policies in Cyrenaica is made by E. E. Evans-Pritchard, who was writing intelligence reports for the British army in 1945. See his book *The Sanasi of Cyrenaica* (Oxford: Oxford University Press, 1949),

160–89. For an overview of the critical Italian scholarships on fascism, see Nicola Labanca, "Internamento Coloniale Italino," in *I campi di Concentratamento in Italia,* ed. Colstantino Di Sante (Milan: Franco Angeli, 2001), 40–67.

17. For a recent study of modern genocide, see Robert Gellately and Ben Kiernin, eds., *The Spector of Genocide: Mass Murder in Historical Perspective* (Cambridge: Cambridge University Press, 2003). For the earliest analysis of genocide (in Libya) in Italian scholarship, see G. Shohat, *Il Colonialismo Italiano* (Turin: Loescher, 1973); Angelo Del Boca, *Gli Italinani in Libia: Dal Fascismo a Gheddafi* (Roma-Barie: Laterza, 1988); and Eric Salerno, *Genocidio in Libia* (Milan: SugarCo, 1979).

18. I dealt with this question ten years ago in chapter 5 of my book *The Making of Modern Libya,* 103–40. For a detailed record of the atrocities of Italian colonialism in Libya, see the book by the exiled Libyan Anti-Fascist Committee, Ha'iyat Tahrir Libia, *'al-Fad'i' al-Humr al-Sud: Min Safahat al-'Isti'imar al-Itali fi Libia* (The Red Black Horrors: Pages of Italian Colonialism in Libya), 2nd ed. (Cairo: Matba'at al-karnak, 1933, 1948).

19. See the collection of essays on the repression of the Libyan resistance and the concentration camps of 1929 to 1939 by Enzo Santarelli et al., eds., *Omar al-Mukhtar,* trans. John Gilbert (London: Darf Publishers Ltd., 1986).

20. See G. Shohat's seminal study, "The Repression of Resistance in Cryenaica (1927–1931)," in Santarelli et al., 73.

21. Enzo Santarelli, "The Ideology of the Libyan 'Reconquest,'" and Shohat, "The Repression," both in Santarelli, *Omar al-Mukhtar,* 11–34 and 72–79.

22. Evans-Pritchard, *The Sanusi,* 189.

23. Roshat, "The Repression," Santarelli, *Omar al-Mukhtar,* 96–7, and his earlier article "Il genocide Cirenaica," *Belfagor* 35, no. 4 (1980): 449–54.

24. Yusuf Salim al-Barghathi, "Al-Mu'taqalat Wa al-Adrar al- Najma 'An al-Ghazwual-Itali" (The concentration camp and its impact on Libya), in *'Umar al-Mukhtar,* ed. Aghail al-Barbar (Tripoli: Center for Libyan Studies, 1983), 146–47.

25. Angelo Del Boca, *Gli Italiani in Libia* II, 175–232.

26. For a biography and full text of Fatima 'Uthamn's poem, see 'Abdalla A. Zagub, "Shahadat al-Mar'a Zamin al-Harb" (A woman as an eyewitness to war), *Al-Thaqafa-al-'Arabiyya* (1980): 85–117.

27. Ben-Ghait, "A Lesser Evil," 140.

28. I am grateful to Dr. Mohammed Jerary who informed me in 1998 about the Italian government's official statement acknowledging some responsibility for colonial crimes. The statement was general and a brief one page. See "Italy-Libya Statement," *BBC News,* July 10, 1998.

29. The Libyan Studies Center has collected oral histories of the colonial period and was advised by historian Jan Vansina of University of Wisconsin, Madison in 1977. I was lucky to have access to this collected oral history at the center's Oral History Archives in Tripoli, Libya.

30. For an introduction to the method of oral traditions and history, see Jan Vansina, *Oral Traditions: A Study in Historical Methodology* (Chicago, IL: Aldine Publishing Company, 1956) and *Oral Traditions and History* (Madison: University of Wisconsin Press, 1985).

31. Al-Maimuni, *Dhiqrayyat Mu'taqal al-Agaila* (Memoirs of the Agail concentration camp) (Tripoli: Center for Libyan Studies, 1995); and Saad Muhammad Abu Sha'ala, *Min Dakhil al-Mu'taqalat* (From inside the concentration camps) (Tripoli: Al-Munshaa al-'Aamma Lilnshar, 1984).

32. Tahir A. al-Zawi, *'Umar al-Mukhtar* (Tripoli: Maktabt al-Firjani, 1970), 166.

33. Al-Maimuni, 68.

34. Salim Muftah Burway al-Shilwi, interviewed by Yusuf al-Barghathi, June 25, 1981, Oral History Archives (Tripoli: Center for Libyan Studies).
35. Ibid.
36. Abd al-'Alli Abu 'Ajailla, *Um al-Khair: The Poet of the Braiga Concentration Camp* (Beneghazi: Al-Maktaba al-Wataniyya, n.d.), 73.
37. Salim Muftah Burway al-Shilwi, interview, 1981.
38. Salim Muftah Burway al-Shilwi, interview, 1981.
39. Al-Barghathi, "Al-Mu'taqalat," 146, al-Maimuni, *Dhiqrayyat*, 71. See also Salim Muftah Burway al-Shilwi, interview, 1981.
40. 'Uthman 'Abdulsalam al-'Abbar, Rabab Adham, ed., in *Oral History*, vol. 29 (Tripoli: Center for Libyan Studies, 1991), 228; and Muhammad 'Abdalqadir al-'Abdalli in Abu-Sha'ala, *Min Dakhil*, 43.
41. Salim Muftah Burway al-Shilwi, interview, 1981.
42. Sa'id 'Abdrahmdn al-Hindiri and Salim Hussain, eds., *Qusa'id al-Jihad* (Poems of the Jihad) vol. I (Tripoli: Center for Libyan Studies, 1984), 180–81.
43. Khalifa Jadallah Madrud, interviewed by Yusuf al-Barghathi, June 24, 1981, Oral History Archives (Tripoli: Center for Libyan Studies).
44. See Hussain Nasib al-Maliki, *Sha'ir Mu'taqal al-Agaila* (The poet of the Agaila concentration camp) (Bengazi: n.d.),
45. Muhammad 'Abdalqadir al-'Abdalli in Abu-Sha'alla, *Min Dahkil*, 48.
46. See A. Abu'Ajailla, *Um al- Khair*, 26–27.
47. For a biography of poet Rajab al-Mnifi, see al-Maliki, *Sha'ir Mu'taqal*, 4, 10, 41–51.
48. For a full text of the epic poem, see al-Malki, *Sha'ir*, 41–51.
49. One positive development after the Italian statement acknowledging some responsibility for the impact of colonization on Libya (1998) is the new collaboration between Italian and Libyan scholars at the Libyan Studies Center in Tripoli and the Instituto Italiano per L'Africa e L'oriente. This collaboration has resulted in three academic conferences; the proceedings of two were published recently—see F. Sulpizi and S. H. Sury, eds., *Primo Convegno su gli Esiliate Libici nel Periodo Coloniale 28–29 Otobre 2000* (Roma: Centro Libico per gli Studi Storici, 2002); and Anna Baladinetti, ed., *Modern and Contemporary Libya: Sources and Historiographies* (Roma: Institito Italiano per L'Africa e L'Oriente, 2003). The Italian government has also promised to help Libya by providing maps of the locations of land mines and information on the fate of many unknown Libyans exiled between 1911 and 1943.

Chapter 5

1. See Catherine Zuckert, "Why Political Scientists Want to Study Literature," *PC: Political Science and Politics* XXVIII, no. 2 (June 1995): 189–90; and Bradford Burns, "The Novel as History: A Reading Guide," in *Latin America*, 6th ed. (Englewood Cliffs, NJ: Prentice Hall, 1994), 355–62.
2. I relied on oral traditions in my study of Libyan social history. See my book *The Making of Modern Libya: State Formation, Colonization and Resistance, 1830–1932* (Albany: State University of New York Press, 1994).
3. For an introduction to the modern Arabic novel, see Roger Allen, *The Arabic Novel: An Historical and Critical Introduction* (Syracuse, NY: University of Syracuse Press, 1982). On modern Libyan literature, see Muhammad Ahmad Atiyya, *Fi al-Adab al-Libi al-Hadith* (Of Modern Libyan Literature) (Tripoli: Dar al-Kitab al-Arabi, 1973); and for a survey of the Libyan novel, see Sammar Ruhi al-Faysal, *Dirasat Fi al-Riwaiya al Libiyya* (Studies in the Libyan Novel) (Tripoli: al-Munsha al-'Ama Lil Nashir Wa al-Tawzi'Wa'Illan, 1983).

4. Ibrahim al-Kuni's focus is the opposite of al-Faqih's. He writes about Libyan society from within. Al-Kuni's novels and short stories are about the Libyan Sahara, its people, animals, and legends, not about urban life like al-Faqih's. For a good introduction to Ibrahim al-Kuni's work, see Ferial J. Ghazoul, "Al-Riwaiya al-Sufiyya Fi al-Adab al- Magharibi" (The Sufi novel in the Maghrib), *ALIF* 17 (1997): 28–53.

5. For an analysis of the impact of oil on Libyan society, see A. J. Allan, *Libya: The Experience of Oil* (Boulder, CO: Westview Press, 1981) and A. J. Allan, ed., *Libya Since Independence* (New York, NY: St. Martin's Press, 1982). On migration to the city of Tripoli, see James Harrison, "Migrants in the City of Tripoli," *Geographical Journal* 57 (July 1967): 415; and Yasin al-Kabir, *al-Muhajurun Fi Trabulus al-Gharb* (Immigrants to the city of Tripoli) (Beirut: Mahad al-Inma al-Arabi, 1982).

6. For an overview of al-Faqih's work, see Lee Rong Jian, "Mazij Min al-Hulm Wa al-Dhakira" (A mixture of memory and imagination), *Adab Wa Naqd*, 1992, 110–13.

7. Despite al-Faqih's subtle criticism of Libyan politics, and his disillusionment with pan-Arab politics, he has served as a Libyan diplomat and has written an epilogue to Qadhdhafi's collection of short stories, *al-Qariyya al-Qariyya, al-Ard al-Ard Wa Intihar Raid al-Fada* (The village the village, the land the land, and the suicide of an astronaut) (Zawiyya: Mataba al-Wahda al-Arabiyya, 1993).

8. See al-Faqih's interview in *Al-Wasat*, no. 815, 1995, 60–65.

9. The character of Fatima in the trilogy is represented in a static way. For an alternative female perspective, see the work of the Libyan writer Sharifa al-Qayadi, *Min Awraqi al-Khasa* (From My Private Papers) (Tripoli: Al Munsha al-Ama Lil Nashir wa -Tawzi Wa Illan, 1986).

10. On the influence of Sufi Islam on Maghribi literature, see Ferial J. Ghazoul, 28–53.

11. See the interview with al-Faqih in *Al-Wasat*, 61, and his essay in *Al-Sharq al-Awsat*, no. 5391, September 1, 1993.

12. On the politics of Islamic laws in Libya, see Ann Elizabeth Mayer, "Legislation in Defense of Arabo-Islamic Sexual Mores," *American Journal of Comparative Law* 27 (1979): 541–59, and her chapter "In Search of Sacred Law: The Meandering Course of Qadhdhafi's Legal Policy," in *Qadhdhafi's Libya, 1969–1994*, ed. Dirk Vandewalle (New York, NY: St. Martin's Press, 1995).

13. Al-Faqih, *Nafaq Tudi'uhu 'Imra Wahida* (A tunnel lit by a woman) (London: Riad al-Rayyes Books, 1991), 256. Hereafter cited as trilogy III.

14. Trilogy III, 235.

15. King Idriss's social base was in the Eastern region, Barqa, while Qadhdhafi was born in the central region, and went to school in the southern region, Fezzan.

16. For a comparative analysis of this genre, see Mary N. Layoun, *Travels of a Genre: The Modern Novel and Ideology* (Princeton, NJ: Princeton University Press, 1990). On Arab intellectuals' views of modernity and identity, see the classical critique by Abdallah Laroui, *The Crisis of the Arab Intellectual: Traditionalism or Historicism?*, trans. Diarmid Cammel (Berkeley: University of California Press, 1976); Issa J. Boulata, "Encounter between East and West: A Theme in Contemporary Arabic Novels," *Middle East Journal* (1976): 49–62; and on Taib Saleh's novel, see Saree S. Makdisi, "The Empire Renarrated: *Season of Migration to the North* and the Reinvention of the Present," *Critical Inquiry* 18 no. 4 (summer 1992): 804–20. For a female Arab perspective on Western cultural encounter, see the Egyptian critic and novelist Radwa Ashour, *al-Rihla, Yawmiyyat Taliba Masriyya Fi America* (The Trip, Days of an Egyptian Student in America) (Beirut: Dar al-Adab, 1983).

17. Al-Faqih, trilogy III, 195.

18. Al-Faqih, *Sa Ahbiqa Madinatun Ukhra*, (I shall present you with another city) (London: Riad al-Rayyes Books, 1991), 150.

Chapter 6

1. Michael Klare, "The Rise and Fall of the 'Rogue Doctrine': The Pentagon's Quest for a Post-Cold War Military Strategy," *Middle East Report* 28, no. 3 (fall 1998): 12–15.

2. For a critical treatment of the image of the Libyan state in official American discourses, consult Mahmoud G. Elwarfally, *Imagery and Ideology in U.S. Policy toward Libya, 1969–1982* (Pittsburgh, PA: University of Pittsburgh Press, 1988); and Stephen R. Shalom, "The United States and Libya Part I: Before Qadhdhafi," *Z* (May 1990), and Part II, June 1990.

3. See Edmund Burke III, "The Image of Moroccan State in French Ethnological Literature," in *Arabs and Berbers: From Tribe to Nation in North Africa*, eds. Earnest Gellner and Charles Micaud (Lexington, MA: D. C. Heath, 1972), 195–99; and Archie Mafeje, "The Ideology of Tribalism," *Journal of Modern African Studies* 9, no. 2 (1971): 253–61.

4. A classical formulation of the segmentary model is E. E. Evans-Pritchard, *The Sanusi of Cyrenaica* (Oxford: Clarendon Press, 1949), 59–60. The most prominent advocate of this model is Ernest Gellner in *Saints of the Atlas* (Chicago, IL: University of Chicago Press, 1969), 35–70. For an application of this model in political science, see John Waterbury, *The Commander of the Faithful* (New York: Columbia University Press, 1970). For a summary of the critiques of the segmentary model, consult David Seddon, "Economic Anthropology or Political Economy: Approaches to the Analysis of Pre-Capitalist Formation in the Maghrib," in *The New Economic Anthropology*, ed. John Clamer (London: Macmillan Press, 1978), 61–107.

5. For an overview of the study of the state, see Lisa Anderson, "The State in the Middle East and North Africa," *Comparative Politics* 20, no. 1 (October 1987); Nazih N. Ayubi, *Overstating the Arab State* (New York: I. B. Tauris, 1998); and Muhammad Elbaki Hermasi, *Al-Mujtama wa al-Dawla fi al-Maghrib al-Arabi* (Society and State in the Arab Maghrib) (Beirut: Center for Arab Unity Studies, 1987). On the cultural roots of the concept of *statelessness* in Libyan society, see John Davis, *Libyan Politics: Tribe and Revolution* (Berkeley: University of California Press, 1987). For a critical analysis of the origins of the state, see Rifaat Ali Abou El-Haj, *Formation of the Modern State* (Albany: State University of New York Press, 1991); Timothy Mitchell, "The Limits of the State: Beyond Statist Approaches and Their Critics," *American Political Science Review* 85 (March 1991): 77–96; and Joel Migdal, "The State in Society: An Approach to Struggles for Domination," in *State Power and Social Forces: Domination and Transformation in the Third World*, eds. Joel Migdal, Atul Kohli, and Vivienne Shue (Cambridge: Cambridge University Press, 1994).

6. Daniel Lerner, *The Passing of Traditional Society: Modernization in the Middle East* (New York: Free Press, 1958). For a critical review of the literature on state formation, see Ali Abdullatif Ahmida, "Colonialism, State Formation and Civil Society in North Africa," *International Journal of Islamic and Arabic Studies* XI, no. 1 (1994): 1–22.

7. Yves Lacoste, "General Characteristics and Fundamental Structures of Medieval North Africa," *Economy and Society* 3 no. 1 (1974): 10–11. For a critique of the Asiatic mode of production, see Perry Anderson, *Lineages of the Absolutist State* (London: Verso, 1985), 462–95. For a critique of orientalism and Eurocentric Marxism, see Brian S. Turner, *Marx and the End of Orientalism* (London: George Allen and Unwin, 1978).

8. For a critique of the modernization theorists' analysis of Islamic ideology, see C. Bernard and Z. Khalizad, "Secularization, Industrialization, and Khomeini's Islamic Republic," *Political Science Quarterly* 94, no. 2 (1979); and Yahya Sadowski, "The New Orientalism and the Democracy Debate," *Middle East Report* 183, no. 4 (July–August 1993): 14–21. On Islamic social movements on the Maghrib, consult

Francios Burgat and William Dowell, *The Islamic Movement in North Africa* (Austin: University of Texas Press, 1993); John Ruedy, ed., *Islamism and Secularism in North Africa* (New York: St. Martin's Press, 1994); and on the Islamic movement in Libya, see George Jaffe, "Islamic Opposition in Libya," *Third World Quarterly* 10, no. 2 (April 1988): 615–31.

9.   Bjorn Beckman, "The Liberation of Civil Society: Neo-Liberal Ideology and Political Theory," *Review of African Political Economy* 20, no. 58 (1993): 20–34; and Ali Abdullatif Ahmida, "Inventing or Recovering 'Civil Society' in the Middle East," *Critique* (spring 1997): 127–34.

10. On populism, see Nicos Mousalis, "On the Concept of Populism," *Politics and Society* 14, no. 3 (1985): 329–48.

11. Ali Abdullatif Ahmida, "The Structure of Patriarchal Authority: An Interpretive Essay of the Impact of Kinship and Religion on Politics in Libya (1951–1960) (Master's paper of distinction, University of Washington, Seattle, 1983); and Malek A. Bush-heua, "Al Nizam al Siyasi Fi Libya, 1951–1969" (The political system in Libya, 1951–1969) (Master's thesis, Cairo University, 1977), 157, 179.

12. See William Roy, "Class Conflict and Social Change in Historical Perspective," *Annual Review of Sociology* 10 (1984): 483–506. On the concept of class formation, see Kent Post, "Peasantization and Rural Political Movements in West Africa," *Archives Europennes de Sociologie* VIII, no. 2 (1972): 223–54.

13. Ali Abdullatif Ahmida, *The Making of Modern Libya: State Formation, Colonization, and Resistance, 1830–1932* (Albany: State University of New York Press, 1994).

14. Mahmoud Mamdani, "State and Civil Society in Contemporary Africa: Reconceptu-alizing the Birth of State Nationalism and the Defeat of Popular Movements," *African Development* 15, no. 4 (1990): 70. For a critical treatment of the nation-state as a model, see Basil Davidson, *The Black Man's Burden: Africa and the Curse of the Nation-State* (New York: Times Books, 1992); and Ashis Nandy, "State," in *The Development Dictionary: A Guide to Knowledge and Power*, ed. Wolfgang Sachs (London: Zed Books, 1992), 264–74.

15. Jacques Roumani, "From Republic to Jamahiriyya: Libya's Search for Political Community," *Middle East Journal* 37, no. 2 (1983): 163. Also see Moncef Djaziri's excellent chapter on the historical and cultural roots of the Libyan state, "Creating a New State: Libya's Political Institutions," in *Qadhdhafi's Libya, 1969–1994*, ed. Dirk Vandewalle (New York, NY: St. Martin's Press, 1995), 177–202.

16. See the texts of the two treaties in Majid Khadduri, *Modern Libya: A Study in Political Development*, 2nd ed. (Baltimore, MD: Johns Hopkins University Press, 1968), 363–98; and for superpowers interests in Libya, see Scott L. Bills, *The Libyan Arena: The United States, Britain, and the Council of Foreign Ministers, 1945–1948* (Kent, OH: Kent State University Press, 1995).

17. On the impact of oil on Libya, see John Anthony Allan, *Libya: The Experience of Oil* (Boulder, CO: Westview Press, 1981); Dirk Vandewalle, ed., "The Libyan Jamahiriyya Since 1969," in *Qadhdhafi's Libya*, 3–46; and Stace Birks and Clive Sinclair, "Libya: Problems of a Rentier State." in *North Africa: Contemporary Politics and Economic Development*, eds. Richard Lawless and Allan Findlay (New York, NY: St. Martin's Press, 1984).

18. See M. O. Ansell and I. M. al-Arif, eds., *The Libyan Revolution: A Source book of Legal and Historical Documents* (London: Oleander Press, 1972); Ruth First, *Libya: The Elusive Revolution* (New York and Harmondsworth, England: Penguin, 1974). On Qadhdhafi's biography, see Mirella Bianco, *Gadafi: Voice from the Desert* (London: Longman, 1974); and Musa M. Kousa, "The Political Leader and His Social Background: Mu'ammar Qadhdhafi, the Libyan Leader" (Master's thesis, Michigan State University, 1978). On his ideas, see *Asijil al-Qawmi* (The national record),

vols. 1–25 (Tripoli: Markaz al-Thaqafa al-Qawmiyya, 1969–1994); and Muammar Qadhdhafi, *The Green Book*, 3 vols. (Tripoli: The Green Book Center, 1980).

19.   Stace Birks and Clive Sinclair, "The Libyan Arab Jamahiriyya: Labour Migration Sustains Dualistic Development," *Maghrib Review* 4 (1979): 95–102.

20.   See Rifaat Ali Abou El-Haj, "The Social Uses of the Past: Recent Arab Historiography of Ottoman Rule," *International Journal of Middle East Studies* 5 (1982): 197–98; and Lisa Anderson, "Legitimacy, Identity, and the Writing of History in Libya," in *Statecraft in the Middle East: Oil, Historical Memory, and Popular Culture*, eds. Eric Davis and Nicholas Gavrielides (Miami: Florida International University Press, 1991), 71–91.

21.   Ruth First, "Libya: Class and State in Oil Economy," in *Oil and Class Struggle*, eds. Peter Nore and Terisa Turner (London: Zed Books, 1980); Mustafa Umar al-Tiir, *Al-Tanmiyya Wa al-Tahdith: Nata'j Dirasa Maydaniyya fi al-Mujtama' al-Libi* (Development and modernization: Results of an empirical study of Libyan society) (Tripoli: Mahad al-Inma al-Arabi, 1980); and Muhomed Zahi el-Magherbi, *Al-Mujtama' al-Madani wa al-Tahaul al-Dimuqrati fi Libya* (Civil society and democratic transformation in Libya) (Cairo: Markaz Ibn Khaldun, 1995), 89–108.

22.   Maya Naur, "The Military and Labour Force in Libya: A Research Note from a Spectator," *Current Research on Peace and Violence* 4, no. 1 (spring 1981): 89–99, and Ibrahim B. Dredi, "The Military Regimes and Political Institutionalization: The Libyan Case" (Master's thesis, University of Missouri, Columbia, 1979).

23.   There is only limited information on the conflict inside the RCC and the 1975 coup attempt, with the exception of that from Abd al Mi'im al-Huni, who lives in exile in Egypt. See his memoirs, which were published in *Al Wasat* 178 (August 28, 1995): 10–15.

24.   On the role of multinational oil corporations, see Joe Stork, *Middle East Oil and the Energy Crisis* (New York: Monthly Review Press, 1975), 138–77, Simon Bromley, *American Hegemony and World Oil* (Cambridge, MA: Polity Press, 1991.

25.   Omar I. El Fathaly and Monte Palmer, "Institutional Development in Qadhdhafi's Libya," in *Qadhdhafi's Libya*, ed., Vandewalle, 157–76.

26.   Abd al-Mi'im al-Huni, *Al Wasa* 178 (August 28, 1995): 12–13.

27.   There is no scholarly analysis of the Libyan Chadian war and its impact on the Libyan state. For an American perspective, see Rene Lemarchand, "The Case of Chad," in *The Green and the Black*, ed. Rene Lemarchand (Bloomington: Indiana University Press, 1988), 106–24.

28.   For a critical analysis of the American official ideology, see Michael Klare, *Rogue States and Nuclear Outlaws: America's Search for a New Foreign Policy* (New York, NY: Hill and Wang, 1995).

29.   See Dirk Vandewalle, "The Failure of Liberalization in the Jamahiriyya," in *Qadhdhafi's Libya*, 203–22. On the impact of the sanctions on Libyan economy, see Ibrahim Nawaar, "Al- Hisar wa al-Tanmiyya: Tathir al-'qubat al-Iqtisadiyya 'Ala al-Tanmiyya fi Libya, Iraq, and Sudan" (Sanctions and development: The impact of economic sanctions on development in Libya, Iraq, and Sudan) in *Kurasat Istratijiyya* (Cairo: Al-Ahram Center for Strategic Studies, 1997), 60.

30.   Dirk Vandewalle, ed., "The Libyan Jamahiriyya Since 1969," *Qadhdhafi's Libya*, 35–6.

INDEX

A

agency, xv, xvi, 36
al-'Agaila concentration camp, x, 19, 35, 44, 46, 47, 48, 50
    See also Minifi, Rajab Buhwaish al-; 'Uthman, Fatima
Anderson, Lisa, 2
anti-colonial resistance, 25, 26, 45, 48, 53, 71, 78, 79
    See also Mukhtar, 'Umar al-; Tripolitanian Republic; politics of resistance
Aouzo Strip, 85
Asiatic Mode of Production, 5, 68–70
Awlad Sulayman (tribe), 5, 7, 12, 15, 16, 33, 90
    See also Sufuf; tribal-peasant alliances; Fezzan; Chad
'ayan, 14, 21, 24, 87
    Ottoman, 24, 26
    in Tripolitania, 21

B

Banco Di Roma, 19
Benghazi, 4, 9, 24, 39, 43, 47, 50, 64
Bilad al-Sudan, xiv, 12, 14, 18, 26, 87

C

capitalist, 8, 10, 21–23, 27, 32, 36, 56, 58, 62, 65, 66, 70, 73–75, 78
    pre, 78, 82
Chad, x, xiii, 12, 26, 53, 76, 81, 85
    Lake Chad, 8, 12, 14–16
civil society, xvi, 70, 71, 85

civil war, 5
class formation, 9, 20–22, 24, 25, 32
collaboration, 20, 26, 27, 29, 30, 32, 33, 50
    See also Hassuna Pasha Qarmanli; Muntsair family
Cologhli, 5, 14, 24, 87
colonialism/colonial, x, xiii, xiv–xvi, 2, 8–10, 12, 18–21, 25–27, 29, 30, 32, 33, 35–39, 41–46, 48, 50, 53, 54, 63–65, 68–78, 83–85
    anti, 25, 26, 30, 31, 42, 45, 48, 53, 71, 75, 78–80, 85
    -ists, xiv, 32, 38, 50
    -ization, xiii, 70
    policy, 27, 30, 32, 41
    pre, xiv, 20, 32, 68–71, 73
committees
    Popular, 72, 78, 80, 81
    Revolutionary, 81, 92
    See also Jamahiriya; Qadhdhafi
concentration camps, xv, 31, 33, 36, 37, 39, 40, 41, 43, 46, 47, 53, 89, 90
Cyrenaica (Barqa), 2–7, 9–11, 15, 20, 24, 25, 26, 30–32, 41–45, 47, 64, 73–76

D

Del Boca, Angelo, 40, 44

E

Egypt, xiv, 4, 9, 10, 13, 14, 18, 24, 26, 42, 50, 53, 58, 62, 63, 64, 70, 73, 75–81
El-Hisnawi, Habib Wadaa, 12
European, xiv, 4–8, 13–21, 24–26, 29, 36, 37, 39, 40, 62, 66, 69, 70, 74, 79, 83, 87
Evans-Pritchard, E.E., 6, 40, 41, 44, 69